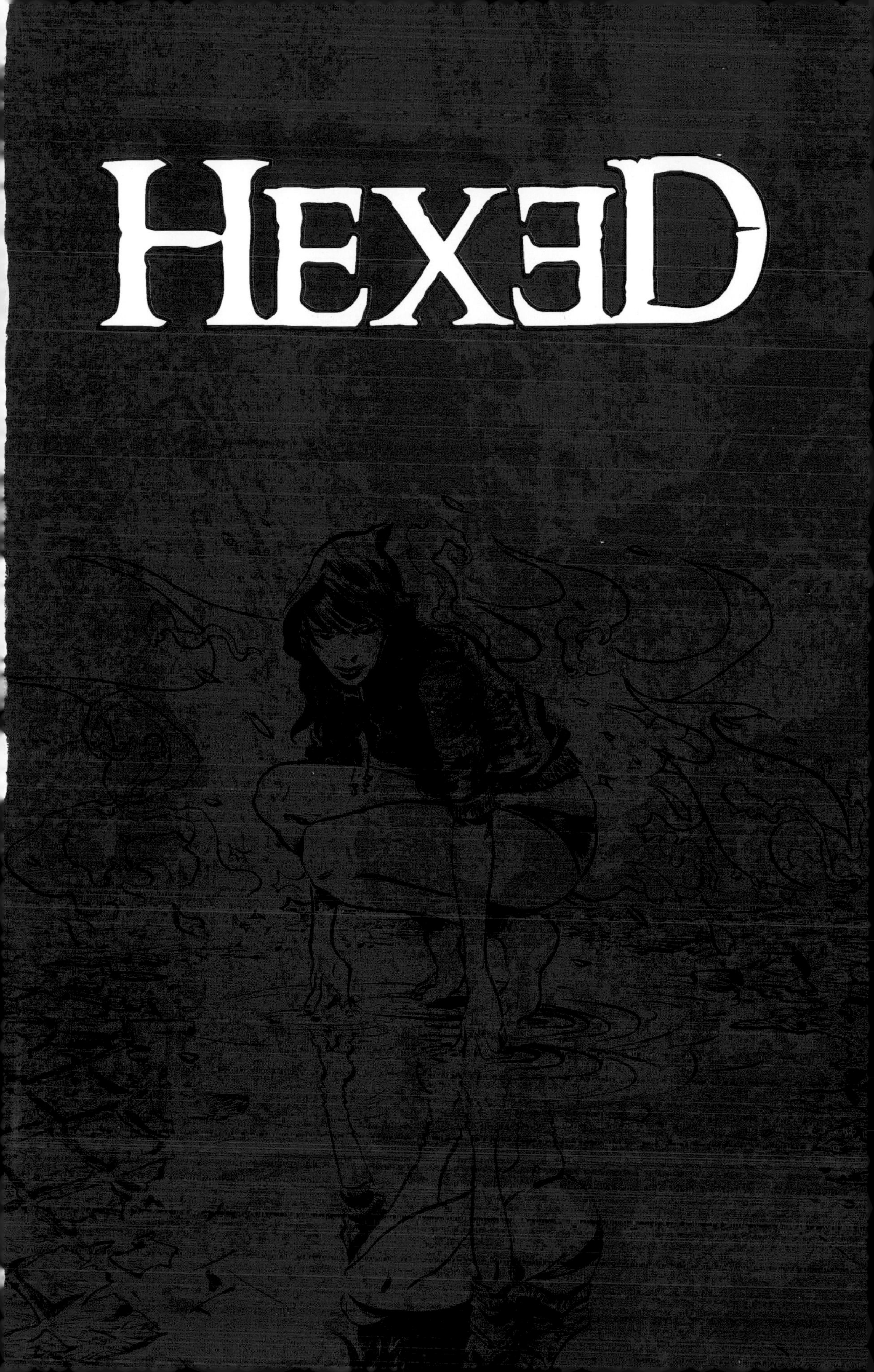
HEXED

ANDREW COSBY
ROSS RICHIE
founders

MARK WAID
editor-in-chief

ADAM FORTIER
vice president,
new business

CHIP MOSHER
marketing &
sales director

MATT GAGNON
managing editor

ED DUKESHIRE
designer

Office of publication: 6310 San Vicente Blvd, Ste 404, Los Angeles, CA 90048-5457.

First Edition: July 2009

10 9 8 7 6 5 4 3 2 1
PRINTED IN KOREA

HEXED

THE DEVIL I KNOW

CREATED AND WRITTEN BY
MICHAEL ALAN NELSON

ART BY
EMMA RIOS

COLORS BY
CRIS PETER

LETTERS BY
MARSHALL DILLON

COVER ART
PAUL POPE

EDITOR
MATT GAGNON

CHAPTER I

WHEREIN LUCIFER GETS A PET AND GOES FOR A SWIM.

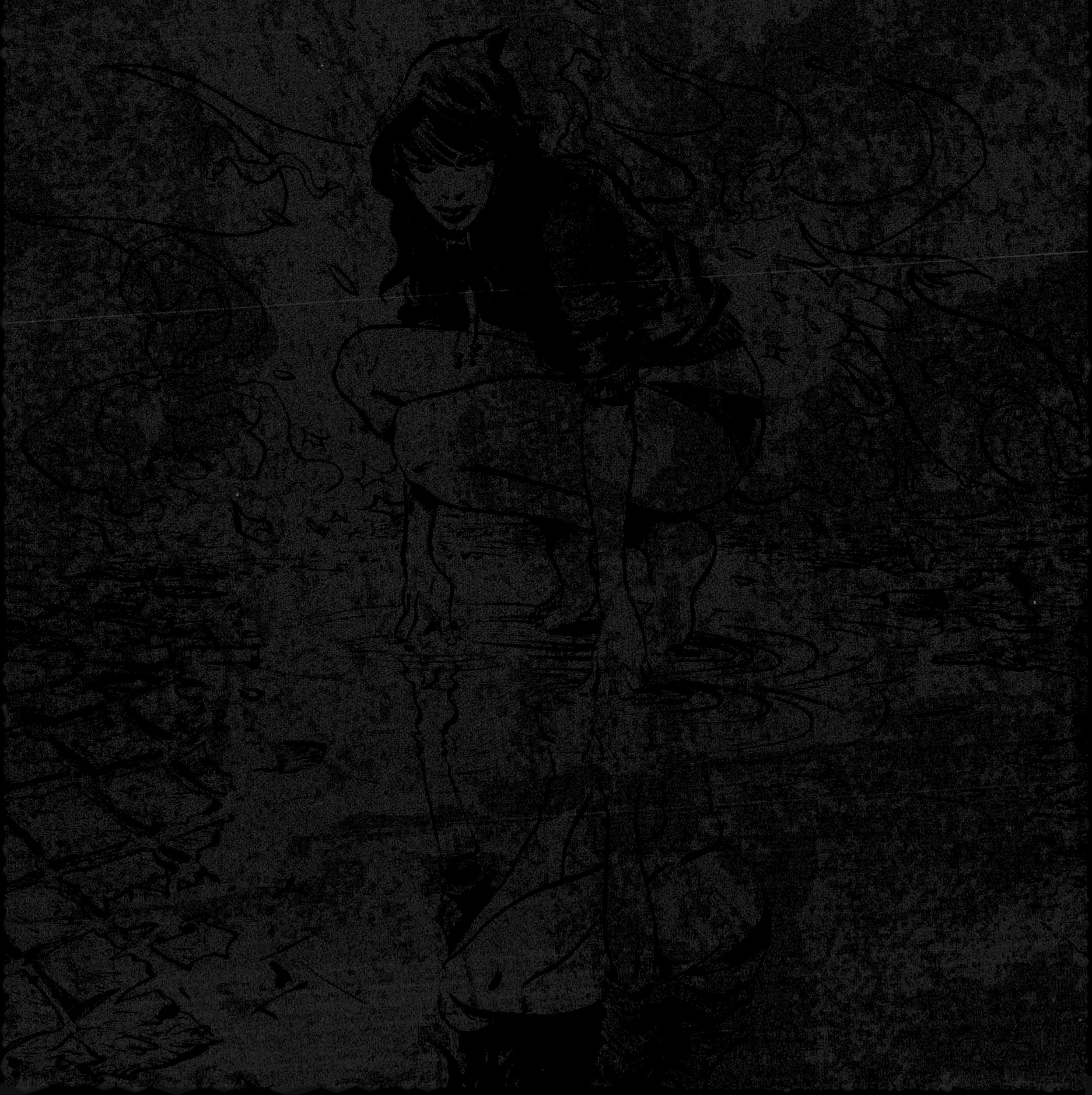

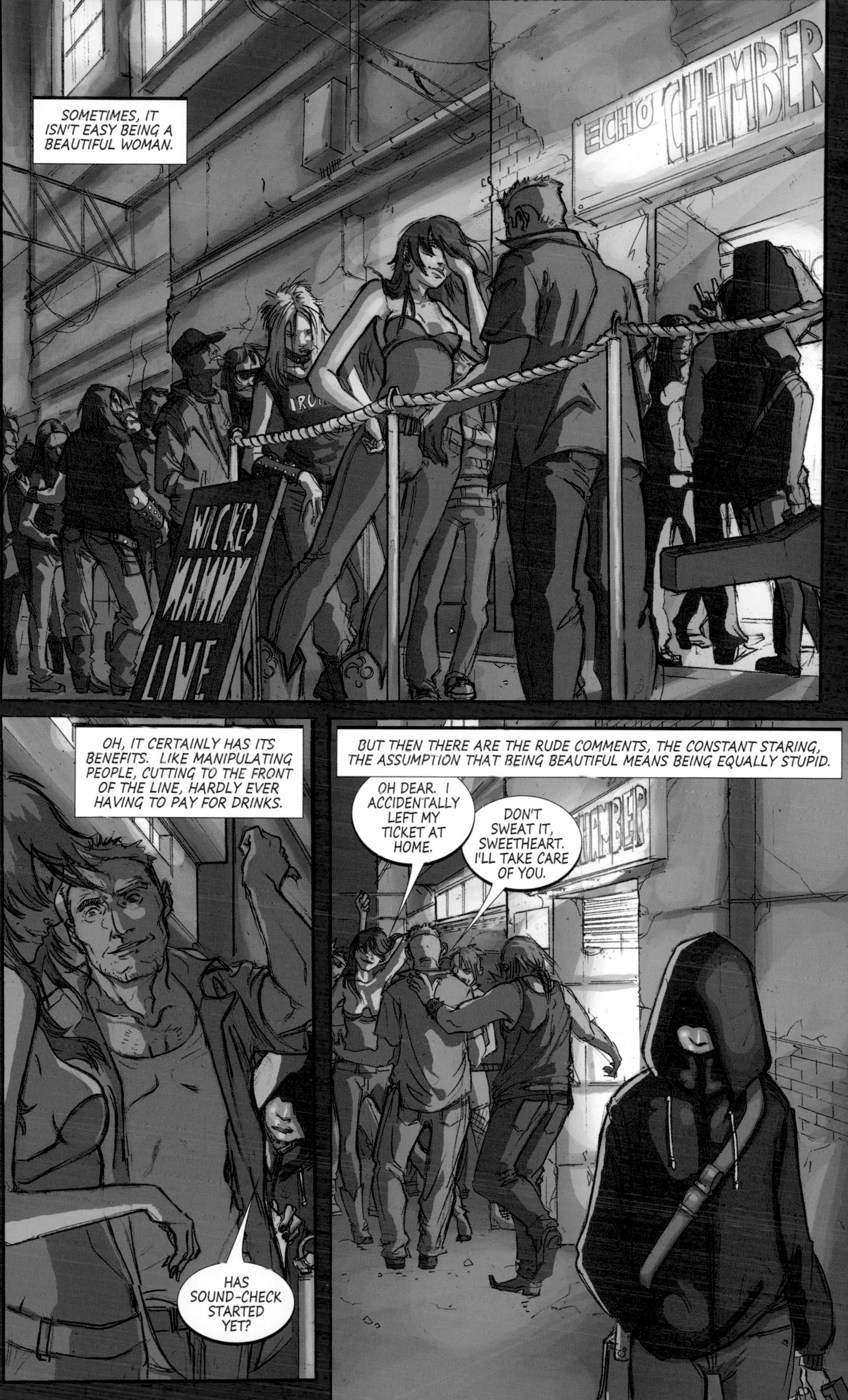
SOMETIMES, IT ISN'T EASY BEING A BEAUTIFUL WOMAN.
ECHO CHAMBER
WICKED MAHHY LIVE
OH, IT CERTAINLY HAS ITS BENEFITS. LIKE MANIPULATING PEOPLE, CUTTING TO THE FRONT OF THE LINE, HARDLY EVER HAVING TO PAY FOR DRINKS.
HAS SOUND-CHECK STARTED YET?
BUT THEN THERE ARE THE RUDE COMMENTS, THE CONSTANT STARING, THE ASSUMPTION THAT BEING BEAUTIFUL MEANS BEING EQUALLY STUPID.
OH DEAR. I ACCIDENTALLY LEFT MY TICKET AT HOME.
DON'T SWEAT IT, SWEETHEART. I'LL TAKE CARE OF YOU.
CHAMBER

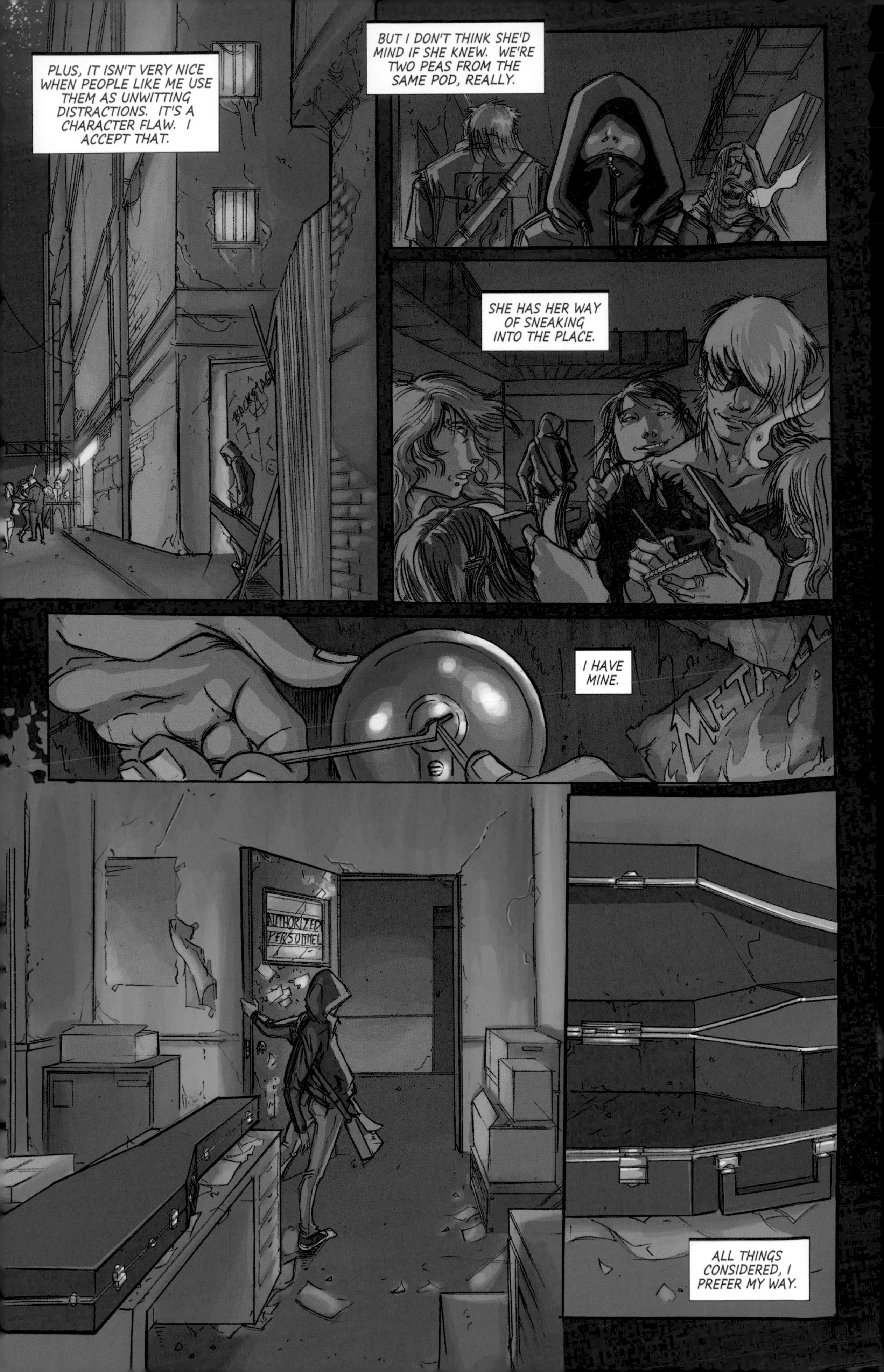
PLUS, IT ISN'T VERY NICE WHEN PEOPLE LIKE ME USE THEM AS UNWITTING DISTRACTIONS. IT'S A CHARACTER FLAW. I ACCEPT THAT.
BACKSTAGE
BUT I DON'T THINK SHE'D MIND IF SHE KNEW. WE'RE TWO PEAS FROM THE SAME POD, REALLY.
SHE HAS HER WAY OF SNEAKING INTO THE PLACE.
I HAVE MINE.
METAL
AUTHORIZED PERSONNEL
ALL THINGS CONSIDERED, I PREFER MY WAY.

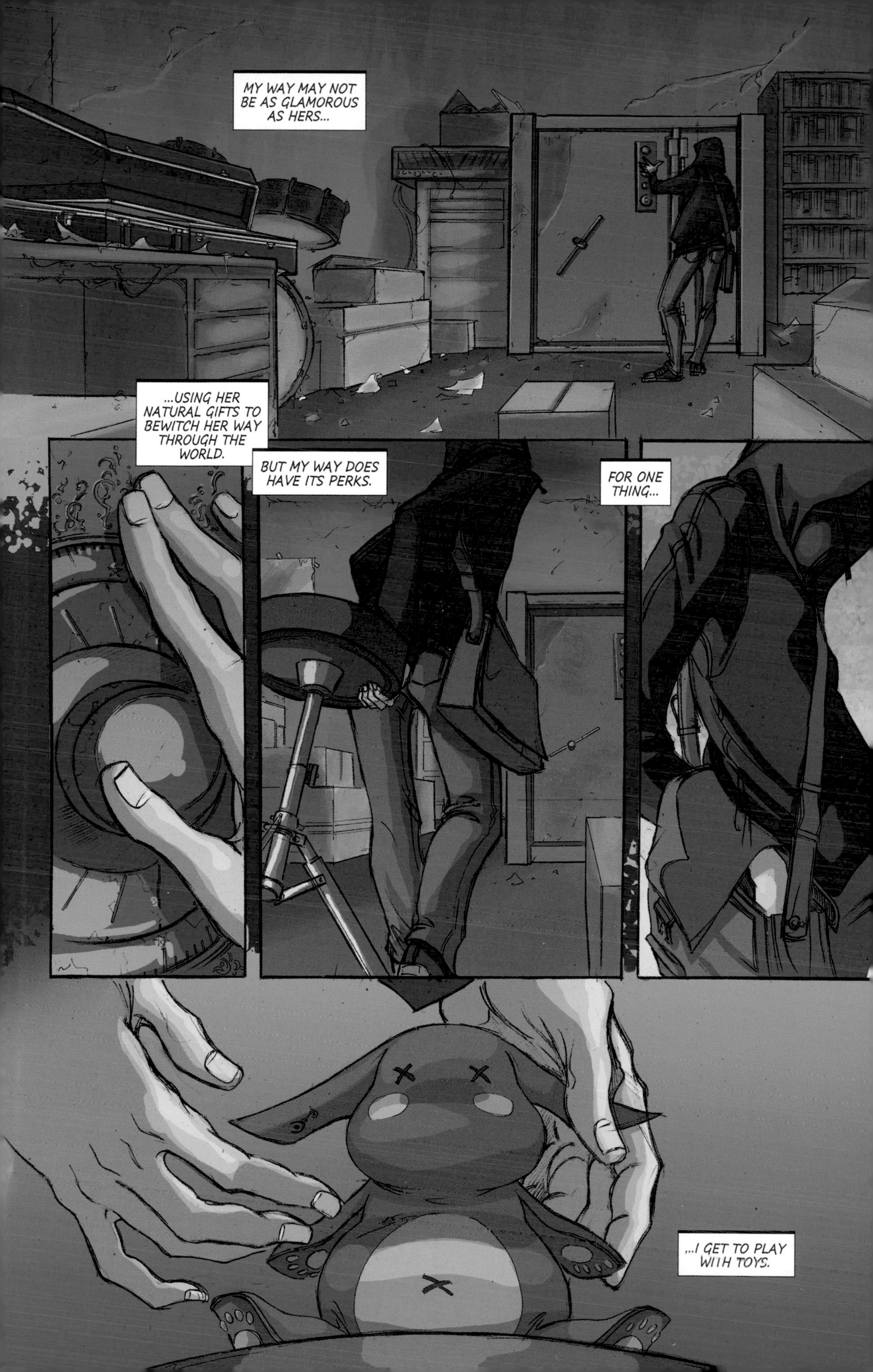
MY WAY MAY NOT BE AS GLAMOROUS AS HERS...
...USING HER NATURAL GIFTS TO BEWITCH HER WAY THROUGH THE WORLD.
BUT MY WAY DOES HAVE ITS PERKS.
FOR ONE THING...
...I GET TO PLAY WITH TOYS.

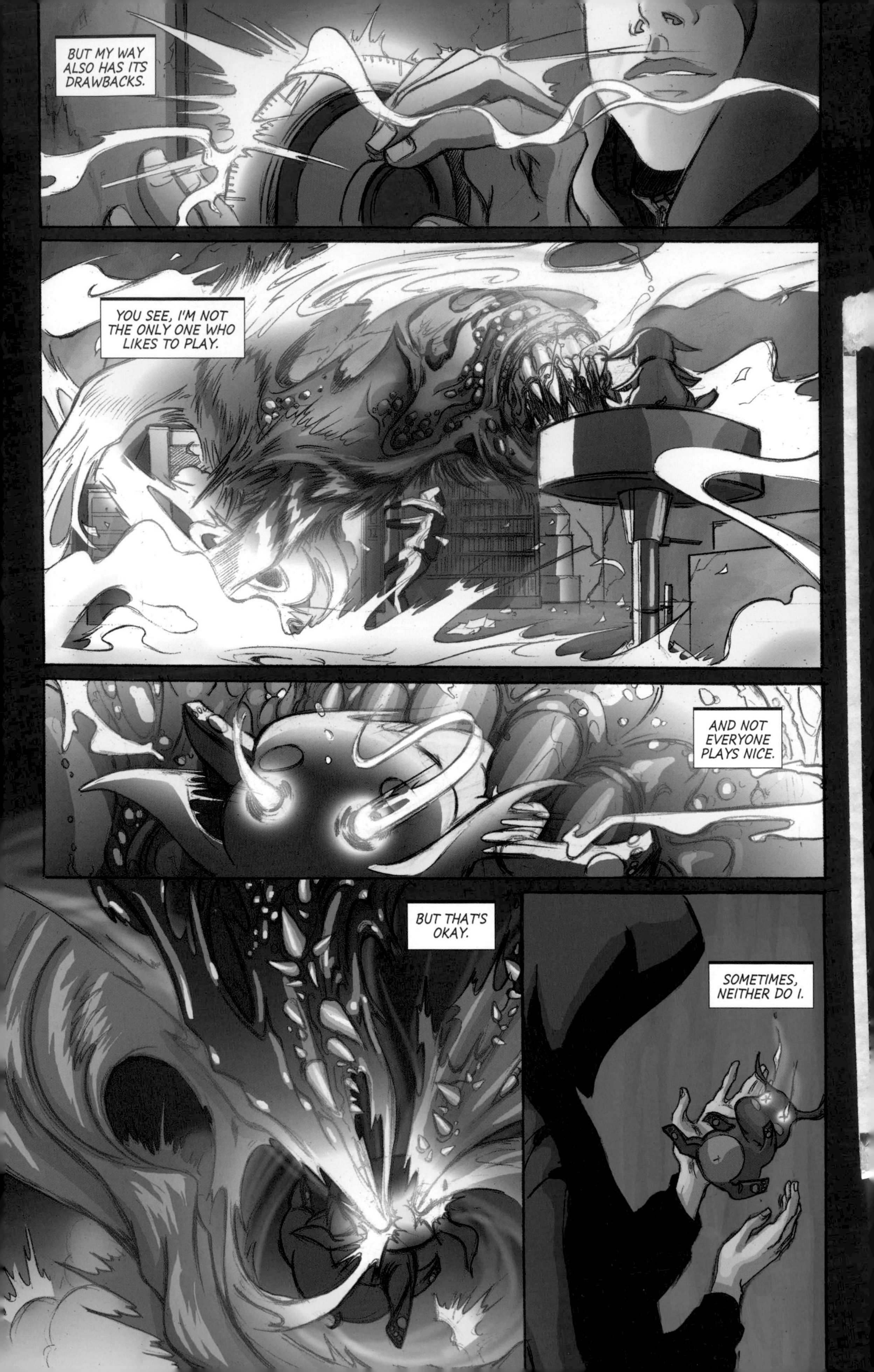
BUT MY WAY ALSO HAS ITS DRAWBACKS.
YOU SEE, I'M NOT THE ONLY ONE WHO LIKES TO PLAY.
AND NOT EVERYONE PLAYS NICE.
BUT THAT'S OKAY.
SOMETIMES, NEITHER DO I.

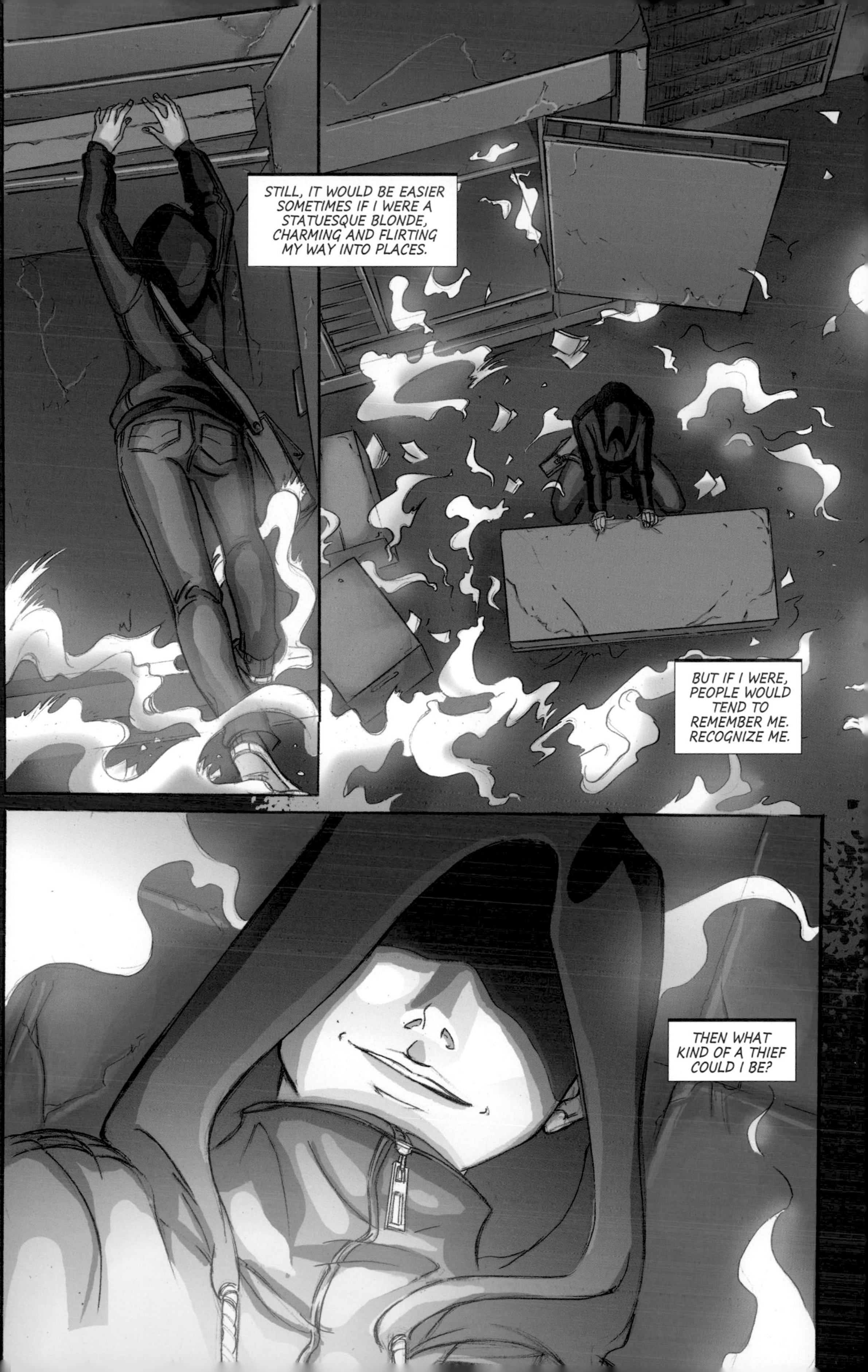
STILL, IT WOULD BE EASIER SOMETIMES IF I WERE A STATUESQUE BLONDE, CHARMING AND FLIRTING MY WAY INTO PLACES.
BUT IF I WERE, PEOPLE WOULD TEND TO REMEMBER ME. RECOGNIZE ME.
THEN WHAT KIND OF A THIEF COULD I BE?

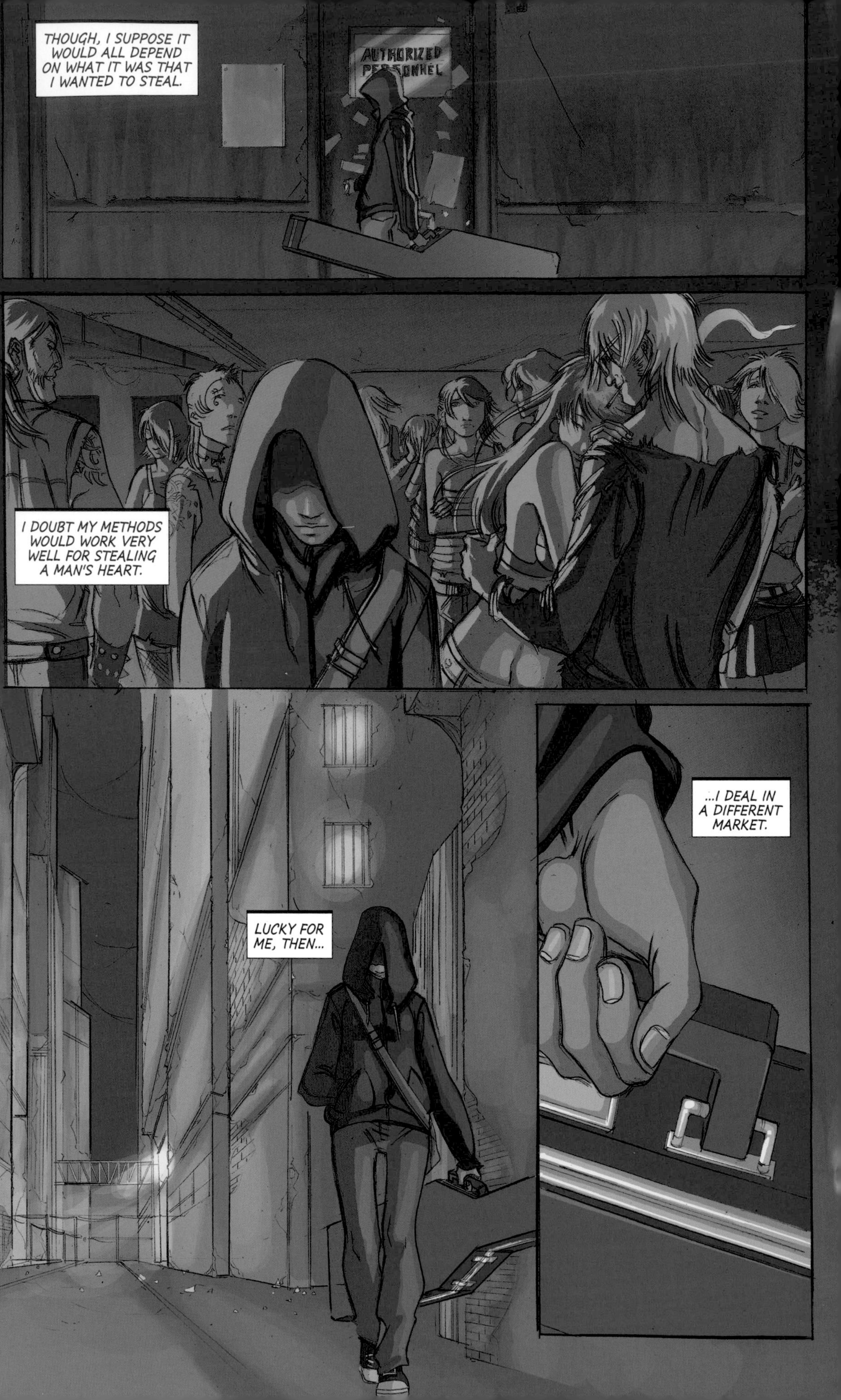
THOUGH, I SUPPOSE IT WOULD ALL DEPEND ON WHAT IT WAS THAT I WANTED TO STEAL.
AUTHORIZED PERSONNEL
I DOUBT MY METHODS WOULD WORK VERY WELL FOR STEALING A MAN'S HEART.
LUCKY FOR ME, THEN...
...I DEAL IN A DIFFERENT MARKET.

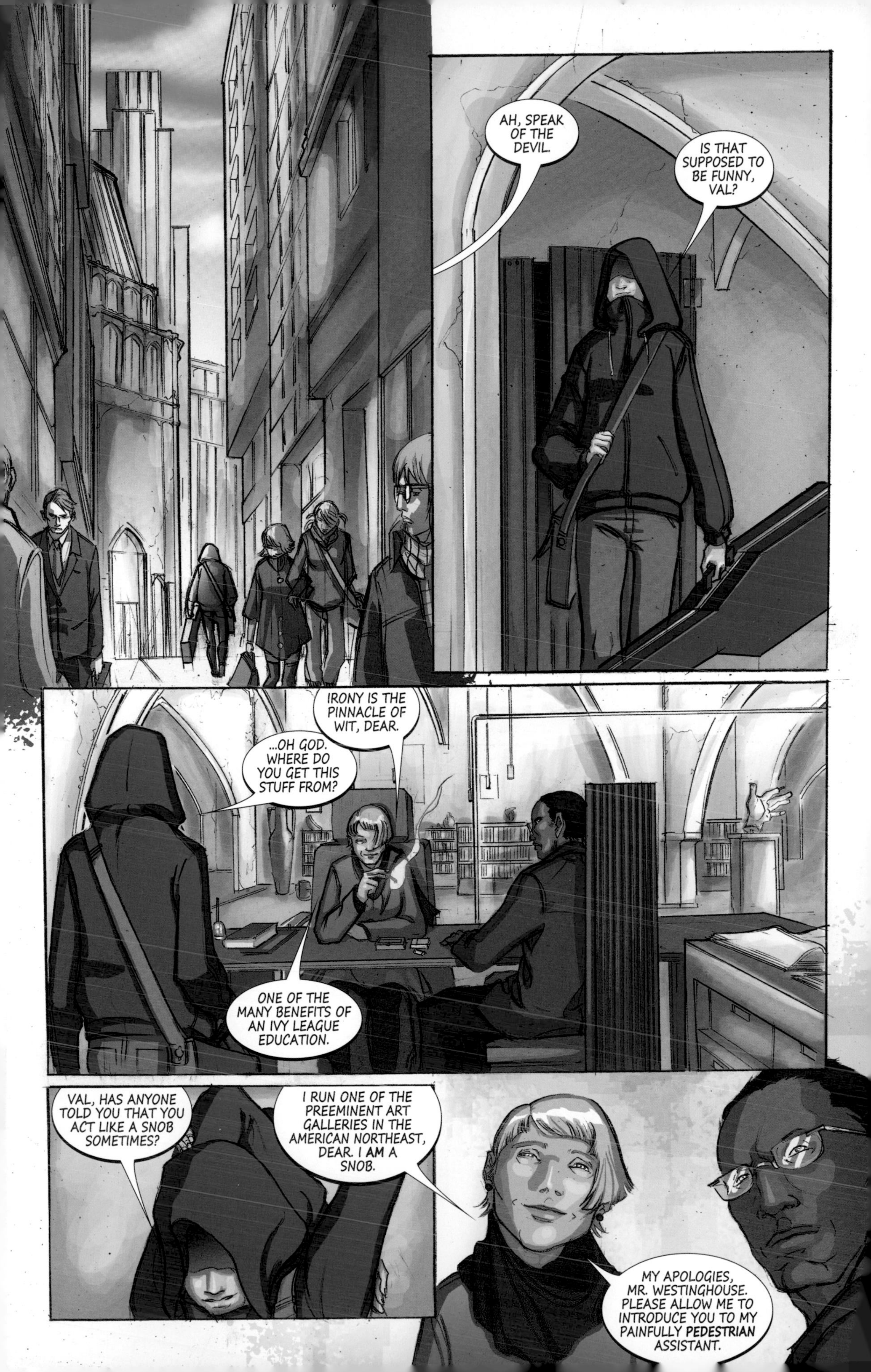
AH, SPEAK OF THE DEVIL.
IS THAT SUPPOSED TO BE FUNNY, VAL?
IRONY IS THE PINNACLE OF WIT, DEAR.
...OH GOD. WHERE DO YOU GET THIS STUFF FROM?
ONE OF THE MANY BENEFITS OF AN IVY LEAGUE EDUCATION.
VAL, HAS ANYONE TOLD YOU THAT YOU ACT LIKE A SNOB SOMETIMES?
I RUN ONE OF THE PREEMINENT ART GALLERIES IN THE AMERICAN NORTHEAST, DEAR. I **AM** A SNOB.
MY APOLOGIES, MR. WESTINGHOUSE. PLEASE ALLOW ME TO INTRODUCE YOU TO MY PAINFULLY **PEDESTRIAN** ASSISTANT.

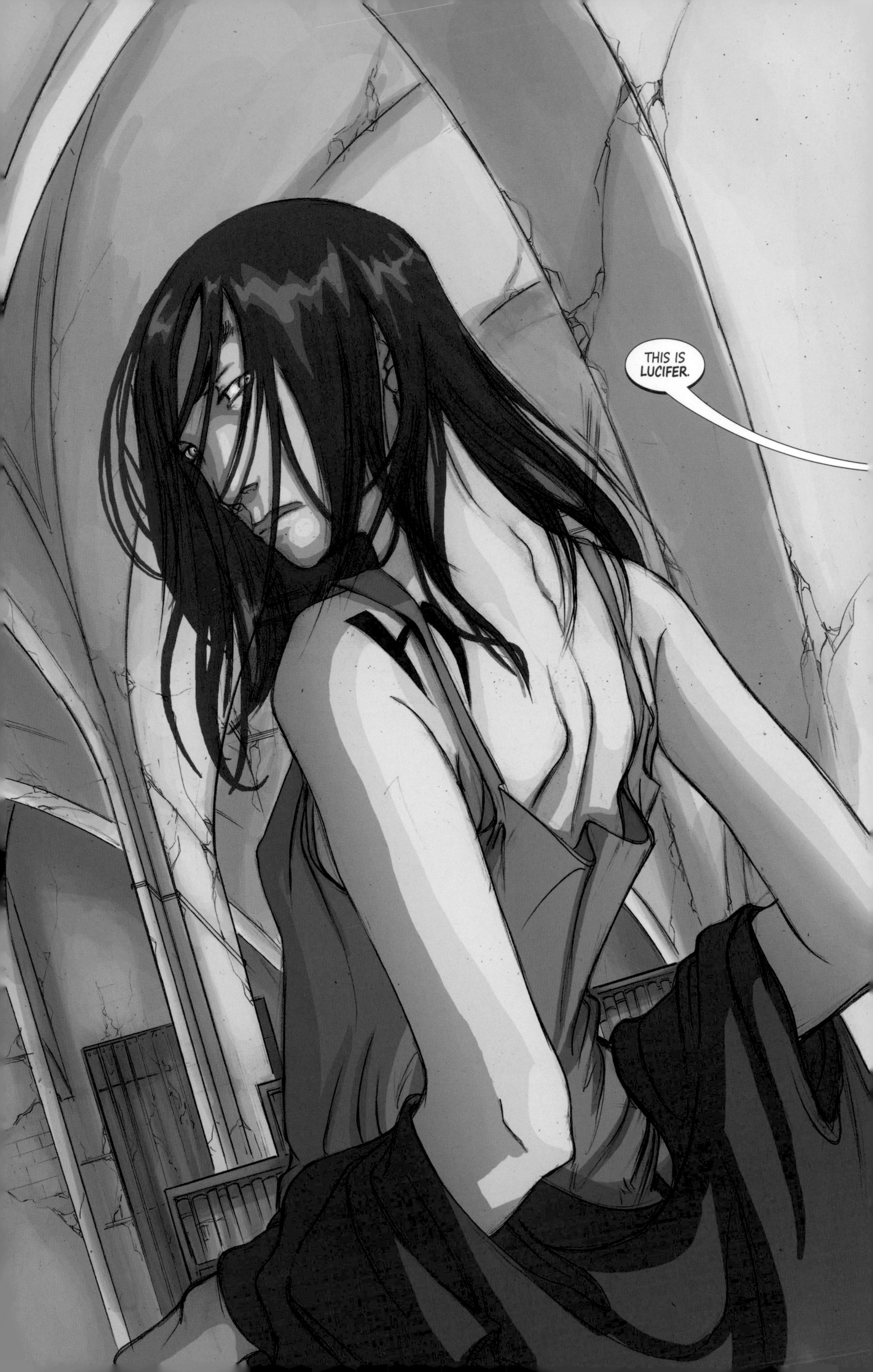
THIS IS LUCIFER.

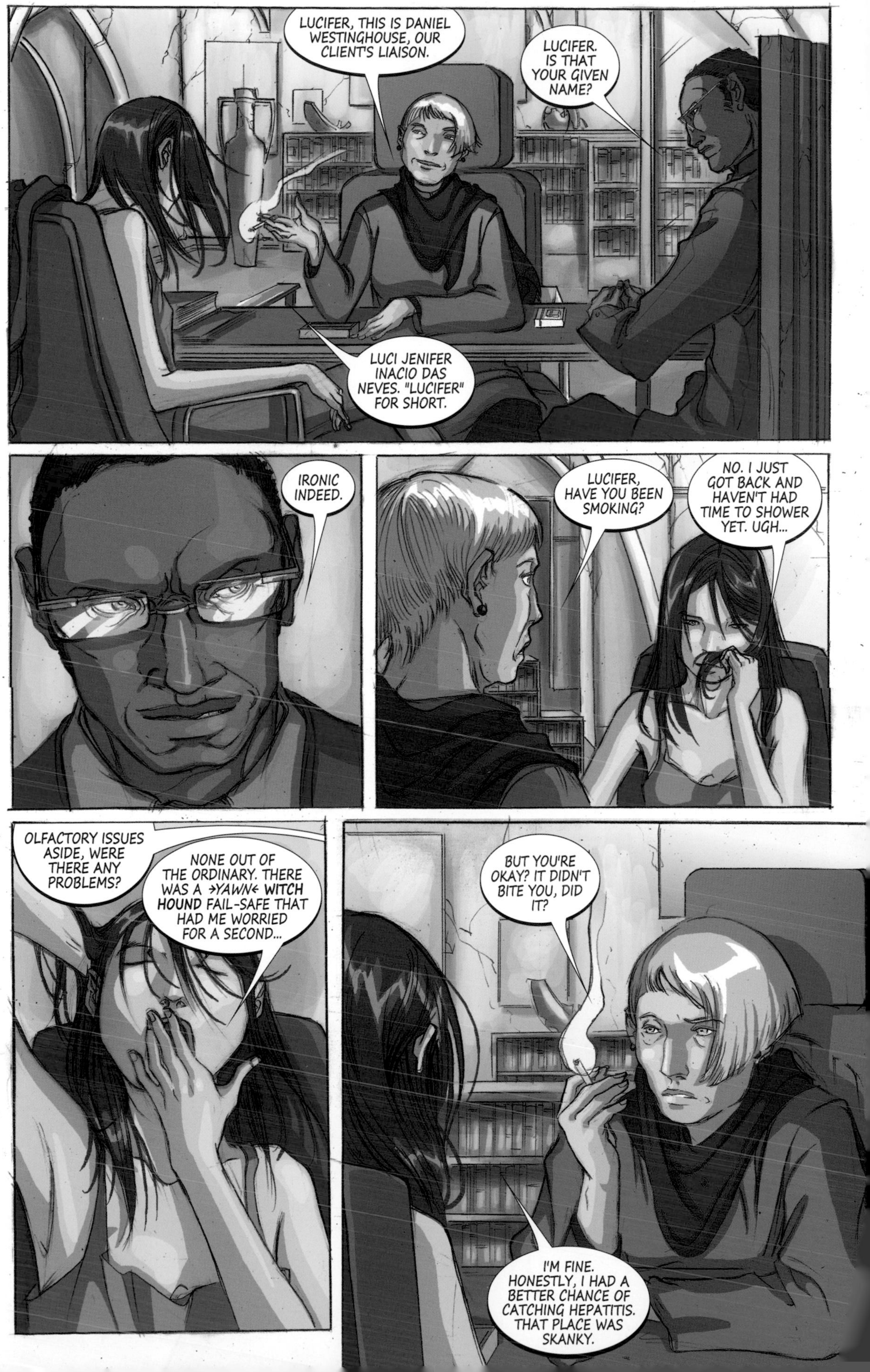
LUCIFER, THIS IS DANIEL WESTINGHOUSE, OUR CLIENT'S LIAISON.
LUCIFER. IS THAT YOUR GIVEN NAME?
LUCI JENIFER INACIO DAS NEVES. "LUCIFER" FOR SHORT.
IRONIC INDEED.
LUCIFER, HAVE YOU BEEN SMOKING?
NO. I JUST GOT BACK AND HAVEN'T HAD TIME TO SHOWER YET. UGH...
OLFACTORY ISSUES ASIDE, WERE THERE ANY PROBLEMS?
NONE OUT OF THE ORDINARY. THERE WAS A ›YAWN‹ **WITCH HOUND** FAIL-SAFE THAT HAD ME WORRIED FOR A SECOND...
BUT YOU'RE OKAY? IT DIDN'T BITE YOU, DID IT?
I'M FINE. HONESTLY, I HAD A BETTER CHANCE OF CATCHING HEPATITIS. THAT PLACE WAS SKANKY.

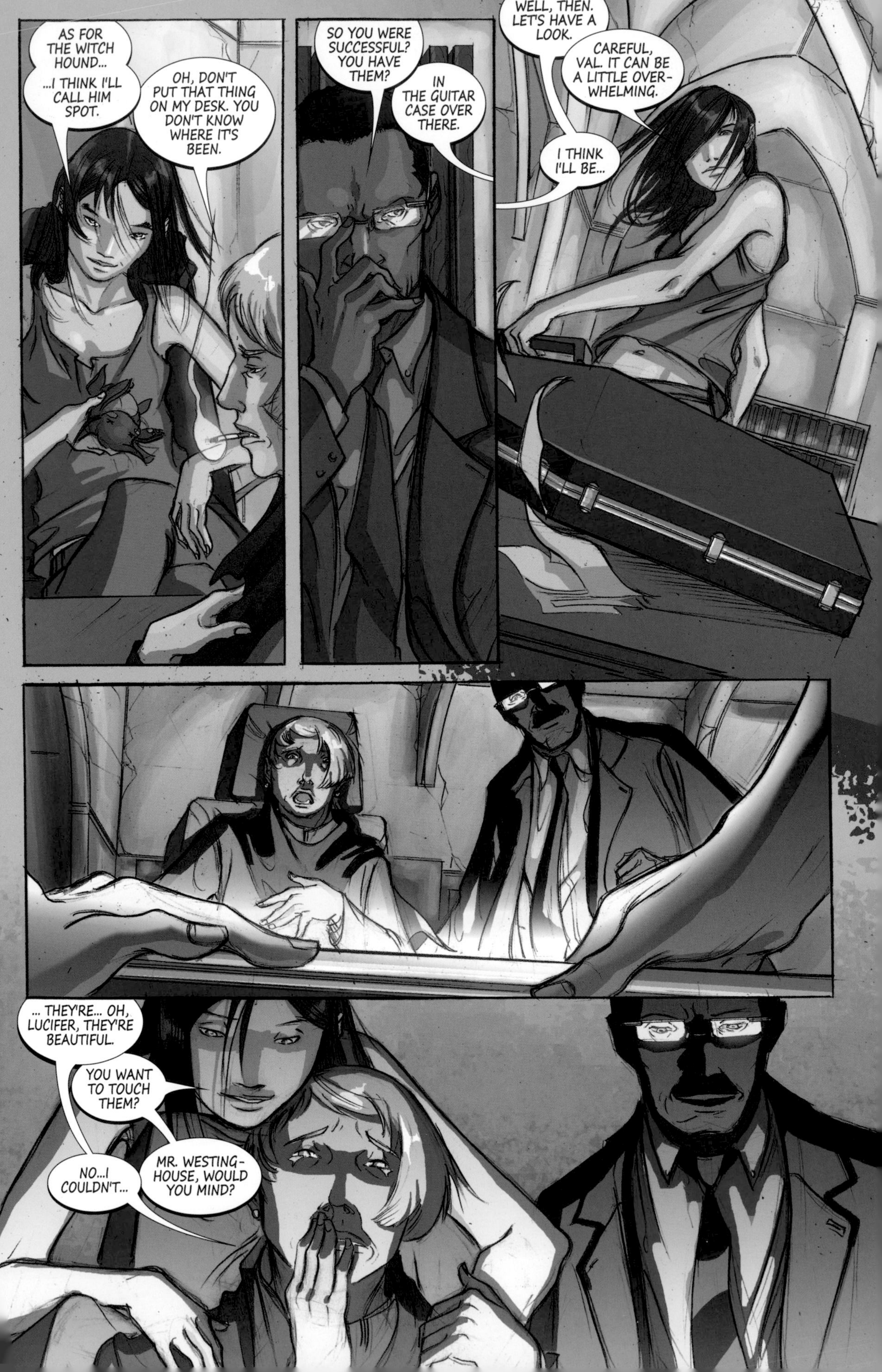
AS FOR THE WITCH HOUND...
...I THINK I'LL CALL HIM SPOT.
OH, DON'T PUT THAT THING ON MY DESK. YOU DON'T KNOW WHERE IT'S BEEN.
SO YOU WERE SUCCESSFUL? YOU HAVE THEM?
IN THE GUITAR CASE OVER THERE.
WELL, THEN. LET'S HAVE A LOOK.
CAREFUL, VAL. IT CAN BE A LITTLE OVER-WHELMING.
I THINK I'LL BE...
... THEY'RE... OH, LUCIFER, THEY'RE BEAUTIFUL.
YOU WANT TO TOUCH THEM?
NO...I COULDN'T...
MR. WESTING-HOUSE, WOULD YOU MIND?

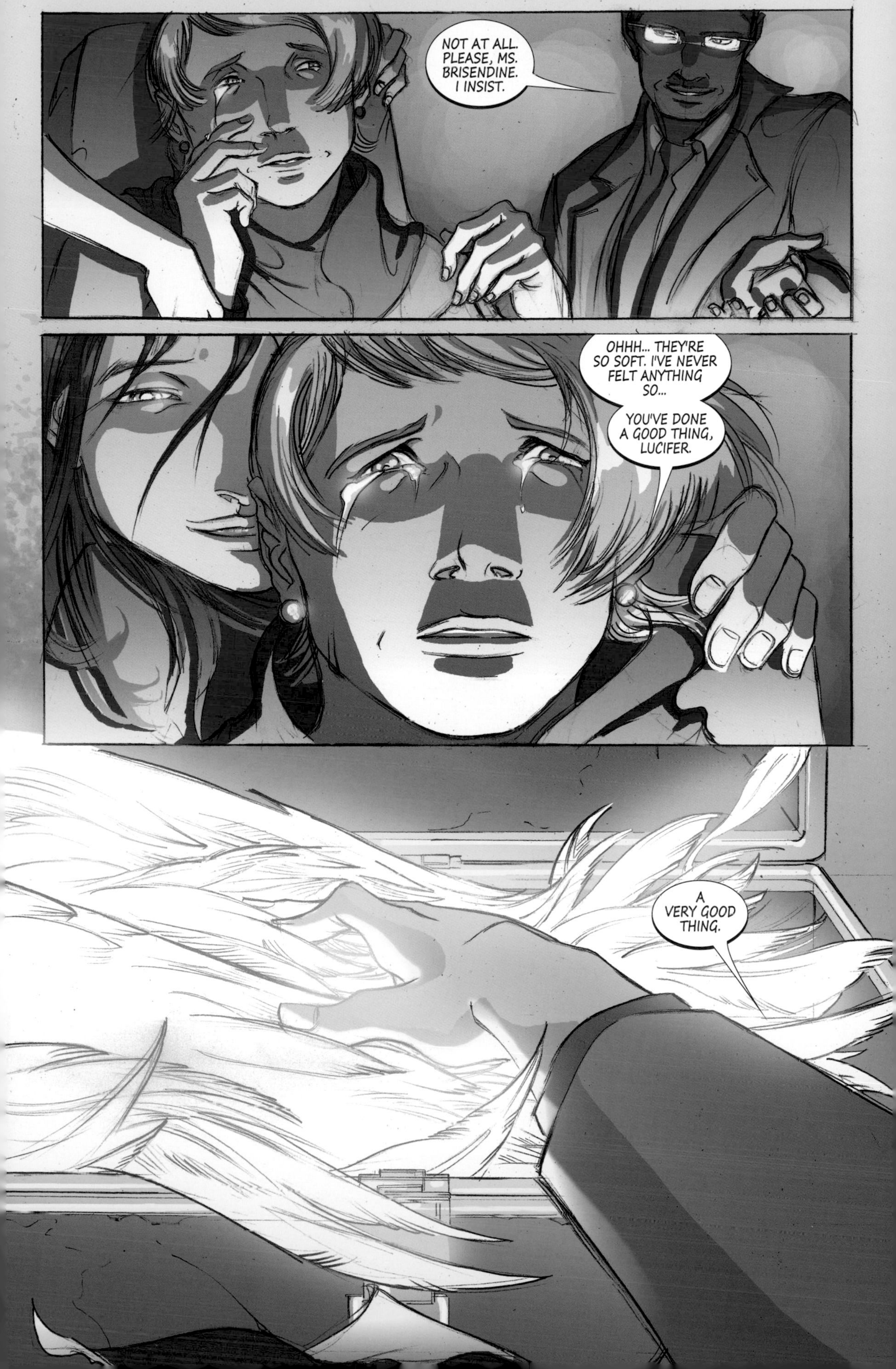
NOT AT ALL. PLEASE, MS. BRISENDINE. I INSIST.
OHHH... THEY'RE SO SOFT. I'VE NEVER FELT ANYTHING SO...
YOU'VE DONE A GOOD THING, LUCIFER.
A VERY GOOD THING.

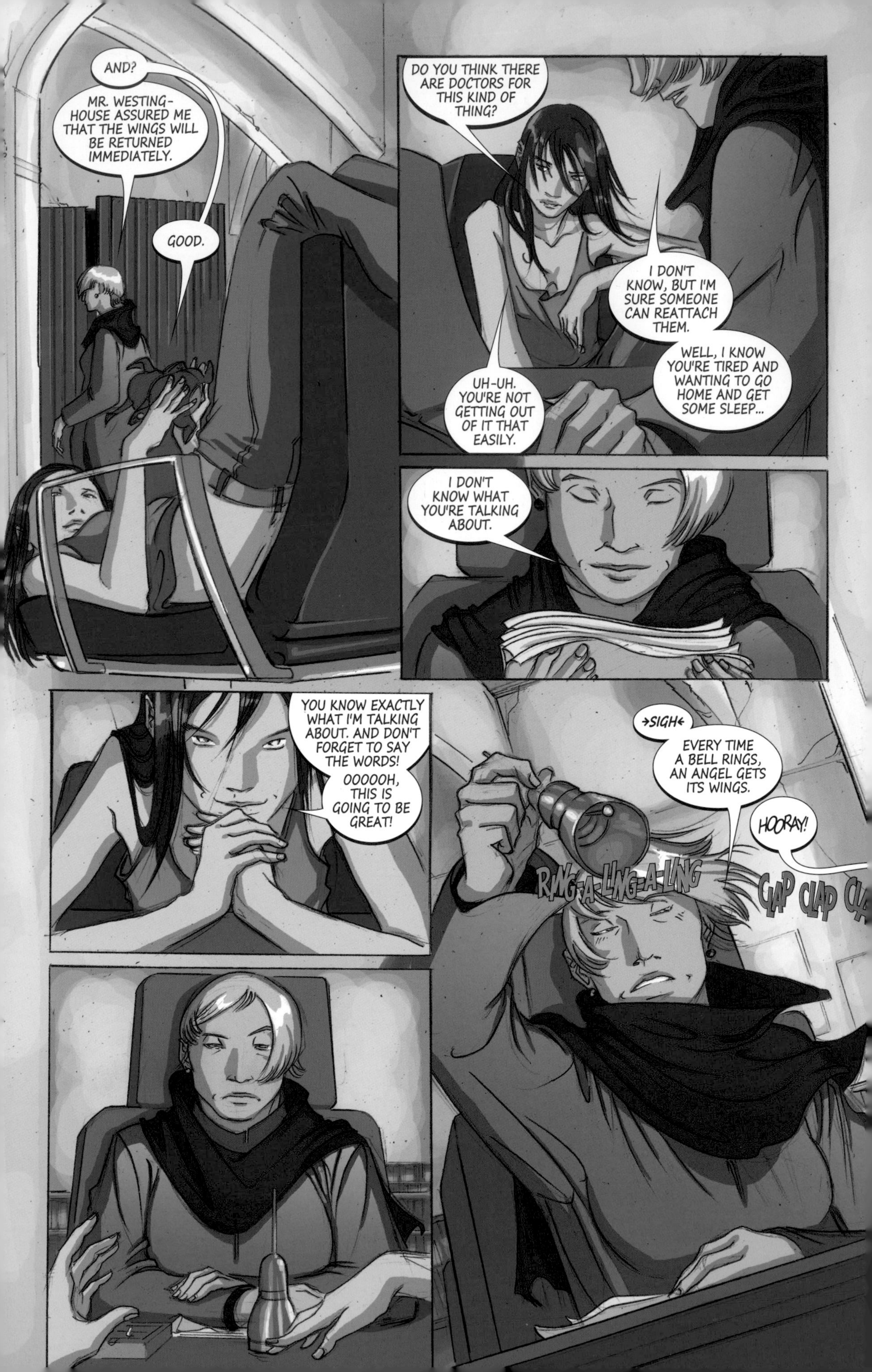
AND?
MR. WESTING-HOUSE ASSURED ME THAT THE WINGS WILL BE RETURNED IMMEDIATELY.
GOOD.
DO YOU THINK THERE ARE DOCTORS FOR THIS KIND OF THING?
I DON'T KNOW, BUT I'M SURE SOMEONE CAN REATTACH THEM.
UH-UH. YOU'RE NOT GETTING OUT OF IT THAT EASILY.
WELL, I KNOW YOU'RE TIRED AND WANTING TO GO HOME AND GET SOME SLEEP...
I DON'T KNOW WHAT YOU'RE TALKING ABOUT.
YOU KNOW EXACTLY WHAT I'M TALKING ABOUT. AND DON'T FORGET TO SAY THE WORDS!
OOOOOH, THIS IS GOING TO BE GREAT!
→SIGH←
EVERY TIME A BELL RINGS, AN ANGEL GETS ITS WINGS.
RING-A-LING-A-LING
HOORAY!
CLAP CLAP CLA

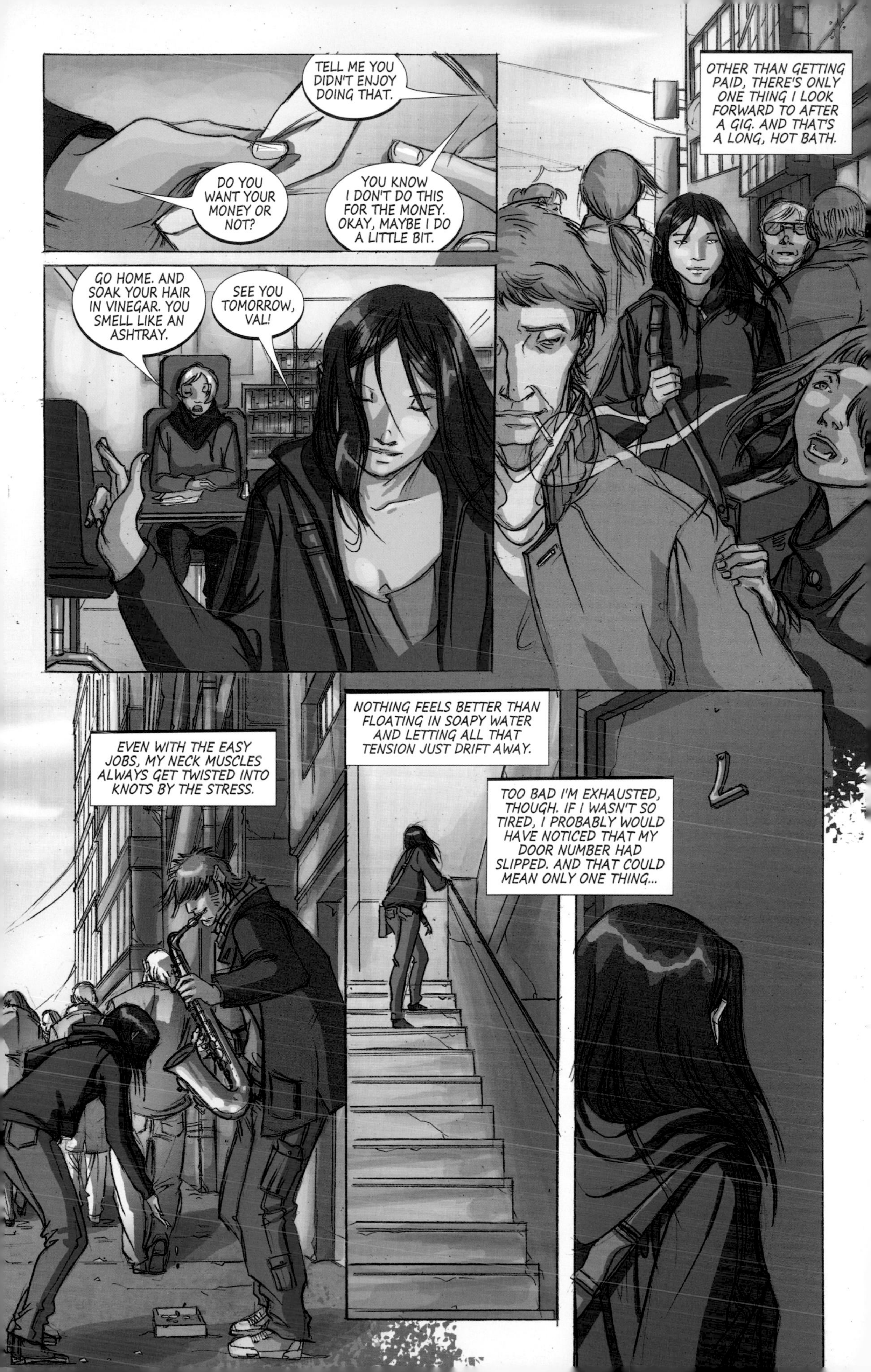

TELL ME YOU DIDN'T ENJOY DOING THAT.
DO YOU WANT YOUR MONEY OR NOT?
YOU KNOW I DON'T DO THIS FOR THE MONEY. OKAY, MAYBE I DO A LITTLE BIT.
OTHER THAN GETTING PAID, THERE'S ONLY ONE THING I LOOK FORWARD TO AFTER A GIG. AND THAT'S A LONG, HOT BATH.
GO HOME. AND SOAK YOUR HAIR IN VINEGAR. YOU SMELL LIKE AN ASHTRAY.
SEE YOU TOMORROW, VAL!
EVEN WITH THE EASY JOBS, MY NECK MUSCLES ALWAYS GET TWISTED INTO KNOTS BY THE STRESS.
NOTHING FEELS BETTER THAN FLOATING IN SOAPY WATER AND LETTING ALL THAT TENSION JUST DRIFT AWAY.
TOO BAD I'M EXHAUSTED, THOUGH. IF I WASN'T SO TIRED, I PROBABLY WOULD HAVE NOTICED THAT MY DOOR NUMBER HAD SLIPPED. AND THAT COULD MEAN ONLY ONE THING...

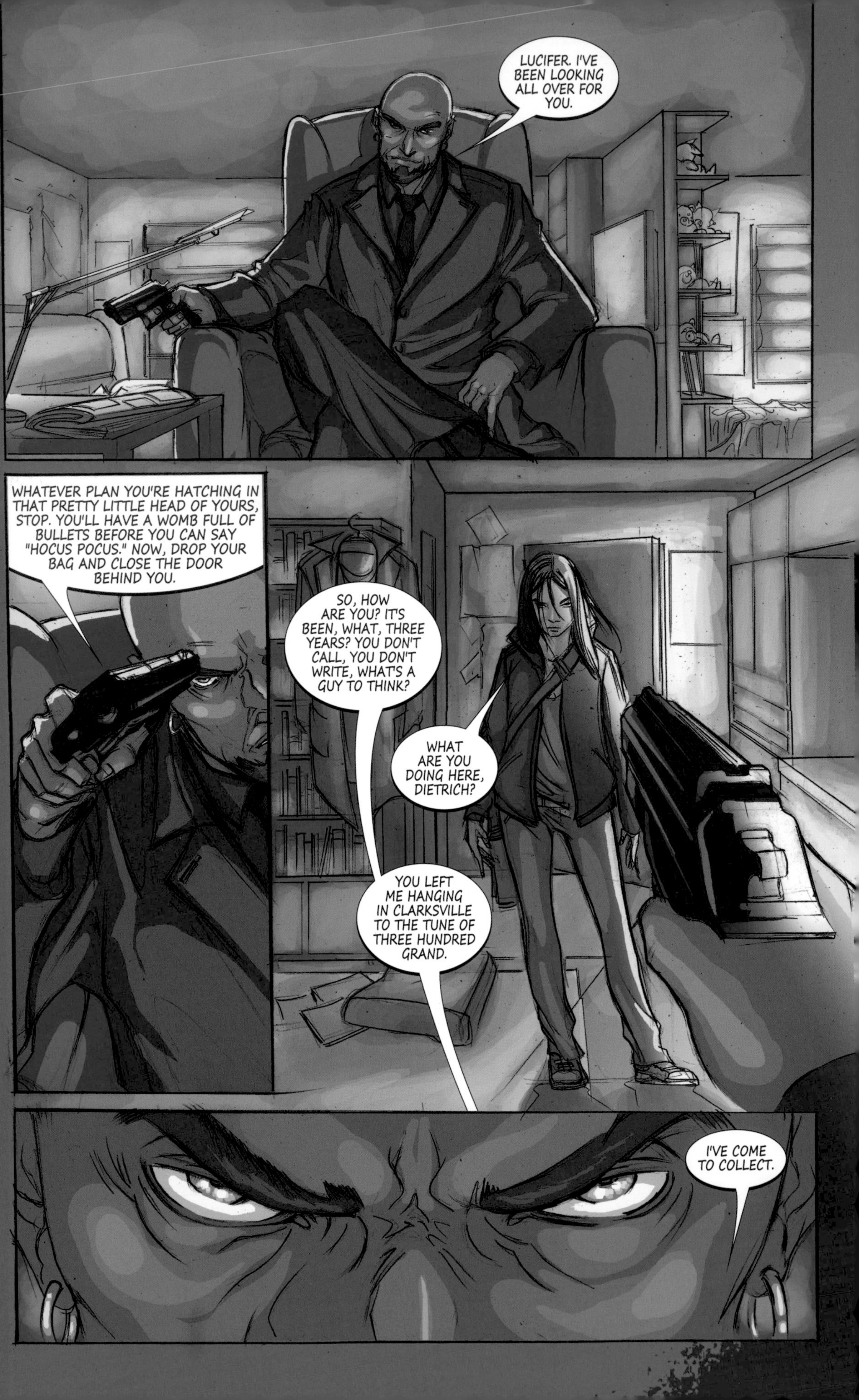
LUCIFER. I'VE BEEN LOOKING ALL OVER FOR YOU.
WHATEVER PLAN YOU'RE HATCHING IN THAT PRETTY LITTLE HEAD OF YOURS, STOP. YOU'LL HAVE A WOMB FULL OF BULLETS BEFORE YOU CAN SAY "HOCUS POCUS." NOW, DROP YOUR BAG AND CLOSE THE DOOR BEHIND YOU.
WHAT ARE YOU DOING HERE, DIETRICH?
SO, HOW ARE YOU? IT'S BEEN, WHAT, THREE YEARS? YOU DON'T CALL, YOU DON'T WRITE, WHAT'S A GUY TO THINK?
YOU LEFT ME HANGING IN CLARKSVILLE TO THE TUNE OF THREE HUNDRED GRAND.
I'VE COME TO COLLECT.

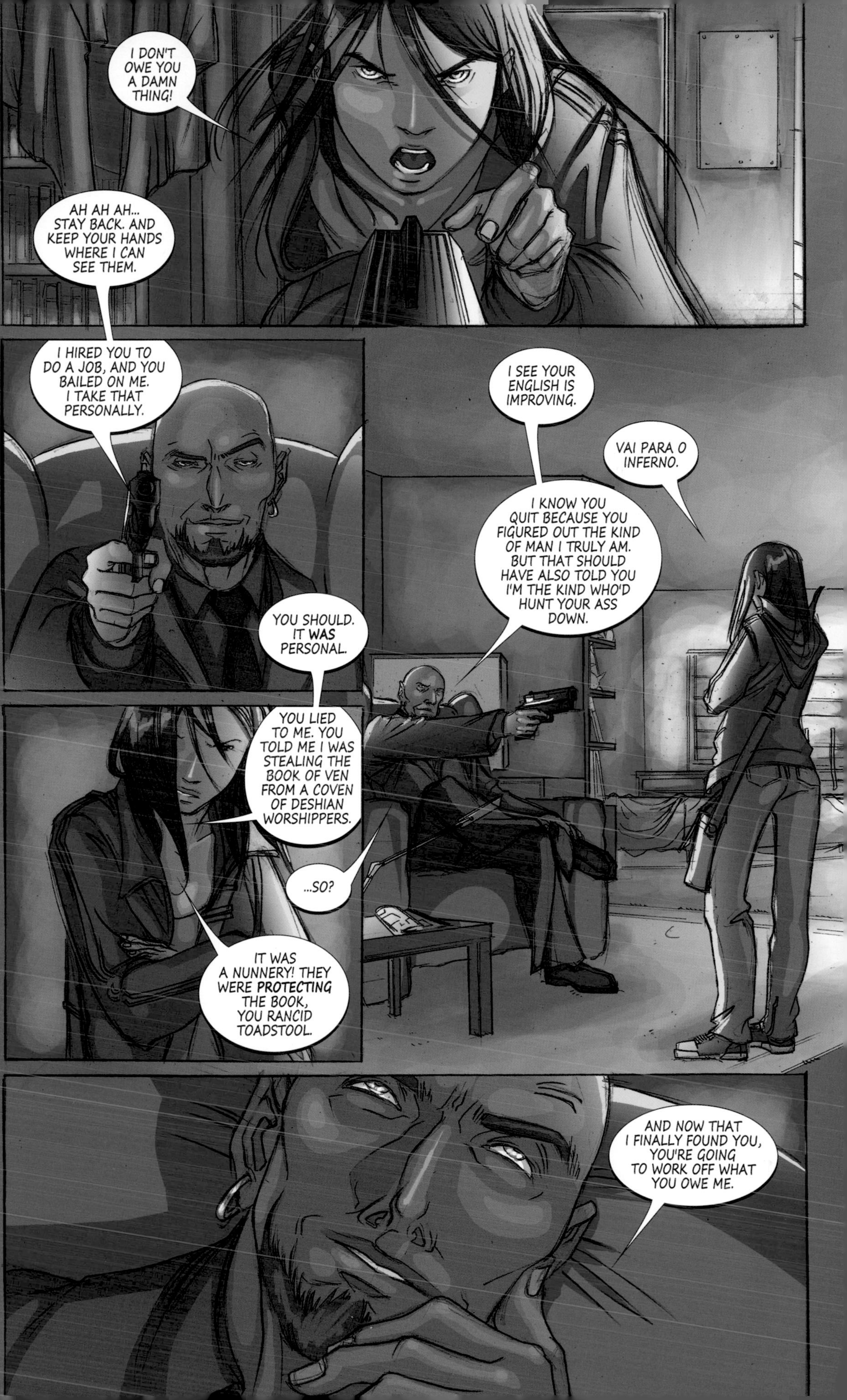
I DON'T OWE YOU A DAMN THING!
AH AH AH... STAY BACK. AND KEEP YOUR HANDS WHERE I CAN SEE THEM.
I HIRED YOU TO DO A JOB, AND YOU BAILED ON ME. I TAKE THAT PERSONALLY.
YOU SHOULD. IT WAS PERSONAL.
I SEE YOUR ENGLISH IS IMPROVING.
VAI PARA O INFERNO.
I KNOW YOU QUIT BECAUSE YOU FIGURED OUT THE KIND OF MAN I TRULY AM. BUT THAT SHOULD HAVE ALSO TOLD YOU I'M THE KIND WHO'D HUNT YOUR ASS DOWN.
YOU LIED TO ME. YOU TOLD ME I WAS STEALING THE BOOK OF VEN FROM A COVEN OF DESHIAN WORSHIPPERS.
...SO?
IT WAS A NUNNERY! THEY WERE PROTECTING THE BOOK, YOU RANCID TOADSTOOL.
AND NOW THAT I FINALLY FOUND YOU, YOU'RE GOING TO WORK OFF WHAT YOU OWE ME.

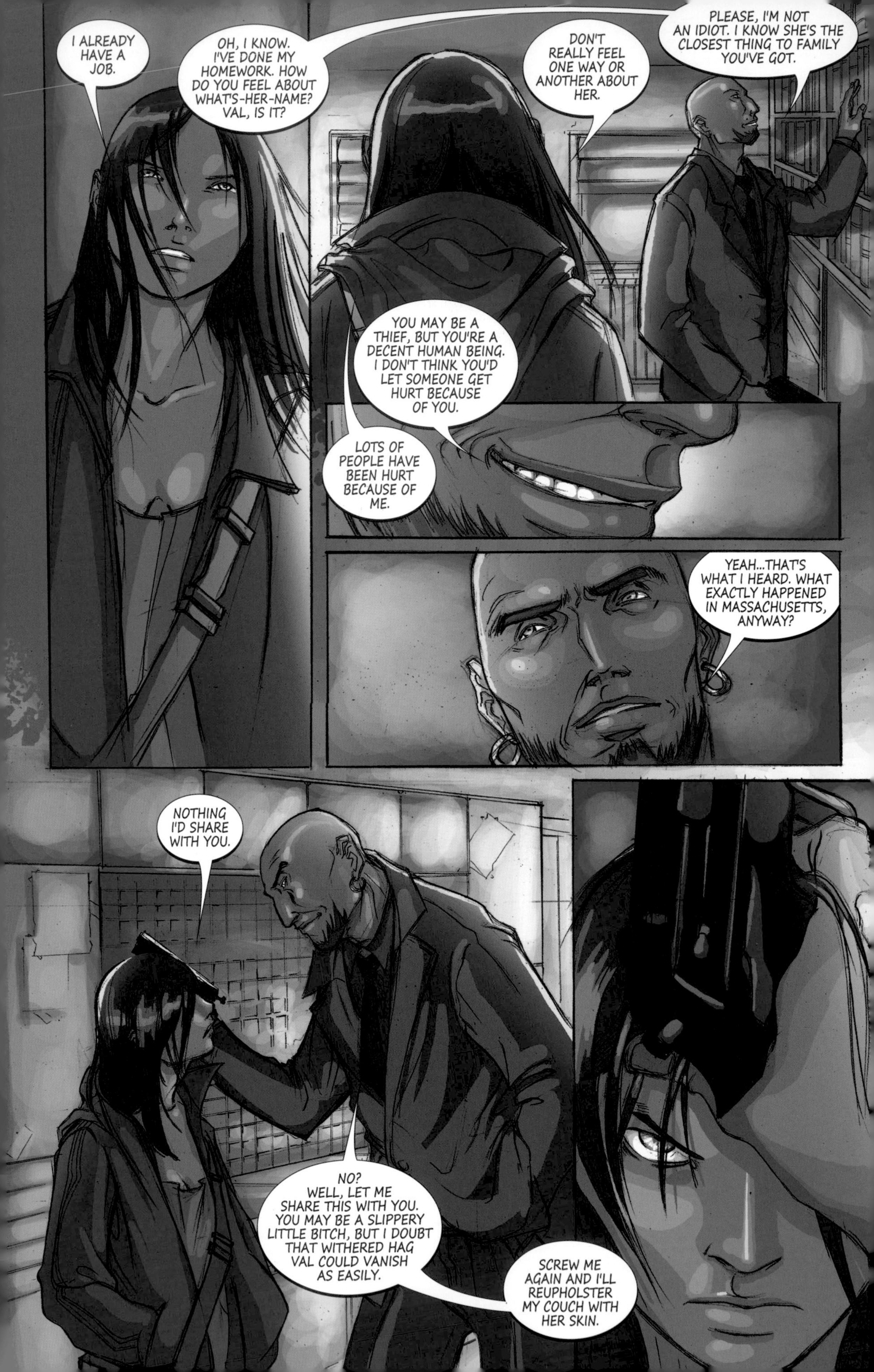
I ALREADY HAVE A JOB.
OH, I KNOW. I'VE DONE MY HOMEWORK. HOW DO YOU FEEL ABOUT WHAT'S-HER-NAME? VAL, IS IT?
DON'T REALLY FEEL ONE WAY OR ANOTHER ABOUT HER.
PLEASE, I'M NOT AN IDIOT. I KNOW SHE'S THE CLOSEST THING TO FAMILY YOU'VE GOT.
YOU MAY BE A THIEF, BUT YOU'RE A DECENT HUMAN BEING. I DON'T THINK YOU'D LET SOMEONE GET HURT BECAUSE OF YOU.
LOTS OF PEOPLE HAVE BEEN HURT BECAUSE OF ME.
YEAH...THAT'S WHAT I HEARD. WHAT EXACTLY HAPPENED IN MASSACHUSETTS, ANYWAY?
NOTHING I'D SHARE WITH YOU.
NO? WELL, LET ME SHARE THIS WITH YOU. YOU MAY BE A SLIPPERY LITTLE BITCH, BUT I DOUBT THAT WITHERED HAG VAL COULD VANISH AS EASILY.
SCREW ME AGAIN AND I'LL REUPHOLSTER MY COUCH WITH HER SKIN.

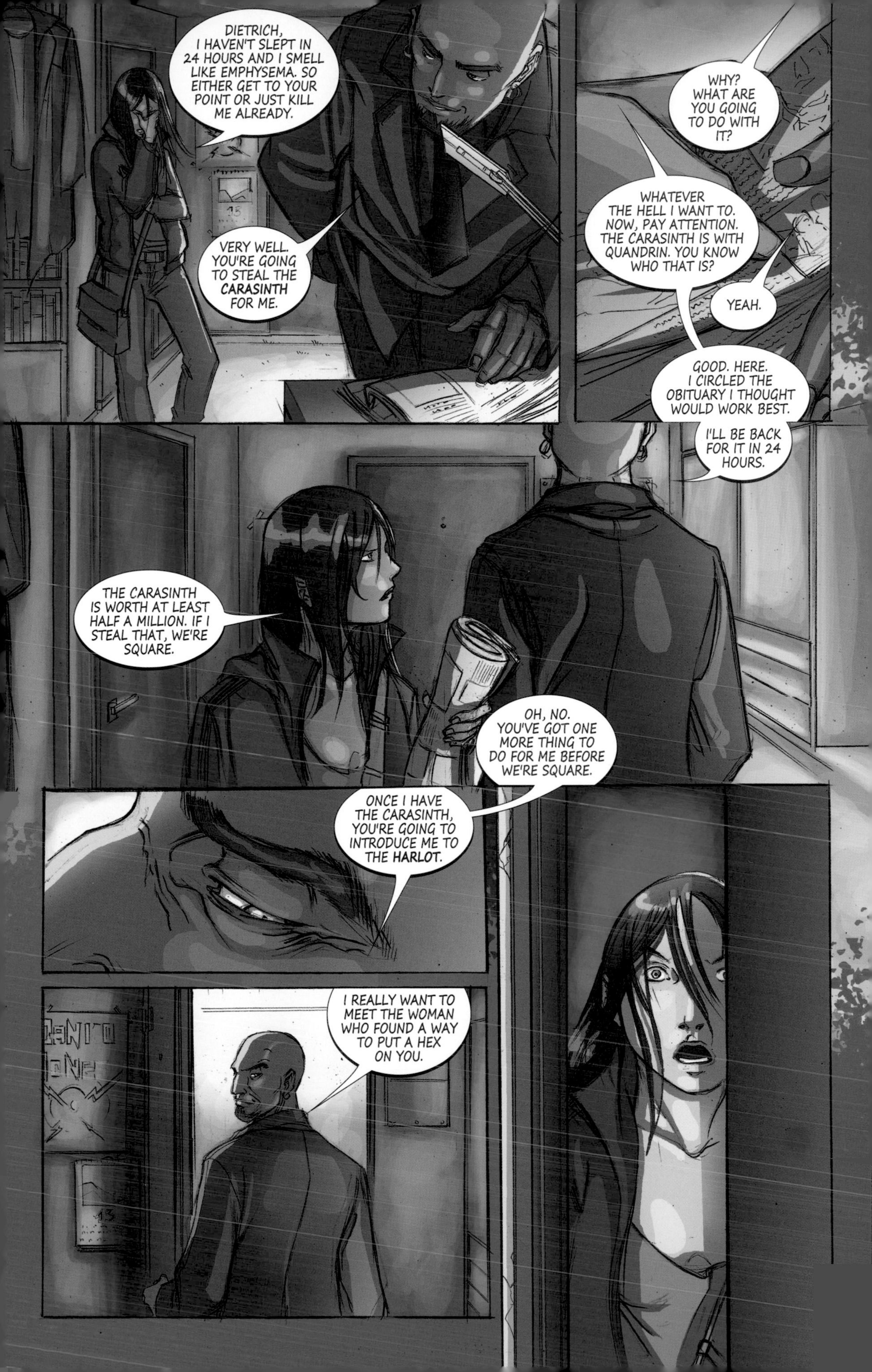
DIETRICH, I HAVEN'T SLEPT IN 24 HOURS AND I SMELL LIKE EMPHYSEMA. SO EITHER GET TO YOUR POINT OR JUST KILL ME ALREADY.
VERY WELL. YOU'RE GOING TO STEAL THE **CARASINTH** FOR ME.
WHY? WHAT ARE YOU GOING TO DO WITH IT?
WHATEVER THE HELL I WANT TO. NOW, PAY ATTENTION. THE CARASINTH IS WITH QUANDRIN. YOU KNOW WHO THAT IS?
YEAH.
GOOD. HERE. I CIRCLED THE OBITUARY I THOUGHT WOULD WORK BEST.
I'LL BE BACK FOR IT IN 24 HOURS.
THE CARASINTH IS WORTH AT LEAST HALF A MILLION. IF I STEAL THAT, WE'RE SQUARE.
OH, NO. YOU'VE GOT ONE MORE THING TO DO FOR ME BEFORE WE'RE SQUARE.
ONCE I HAVE THE CARASINTH, YOU'RE GOING TO INTRODUCE ME TO THE **HARLOT**.
I REALLY WANT TO MEET THE WOMAN WHO FOUND A WAY TO PUT A HEX ON YOU.

ABESTADO! I KNEW I NEVER SHOULD HAVE TAKEN THAT JOB. BUT THAT WAS RIGHT AFTER I LEFT MASSACHUSETTS. I WASN'T EXACTLY THINKING TOO CLEARLY BACK THEN.

I DIDN'T THINK HE WOULD BUY MY BLUFF ABOUT NOT CARING FOR VAL, BUT IT WAS WORTH A SHOT. IF ANYTHING HAPPENED TO HER... OKAY, I HAVE TO FOCUS. I'M JUST TOO DAMN TIRED TO PREP FOR THIS GIG.

WHY DOES HE WANT THE CARASINTH? IF I KNEW, I MIGHT BE ABLE TO FIGURE OUT A WAY OUT OF THIS MESS WITHOUT GETTING VAL, OR MYSELF, KILLED. BUT THAT'S NOT WHAT WORRIES ME MOST...

...HOW DOES HE KNOW ABOUT THE HARLOT?

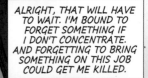

ALRIGHT, THAT WILL HAVE TO WAIT. I'M BOUND TO FORGET SOMETHING IF I DON'T CONCENTRATE. AND FORGETTING TO BRING SOMETHING ON THIS JOB COULD GET ME KILLED.

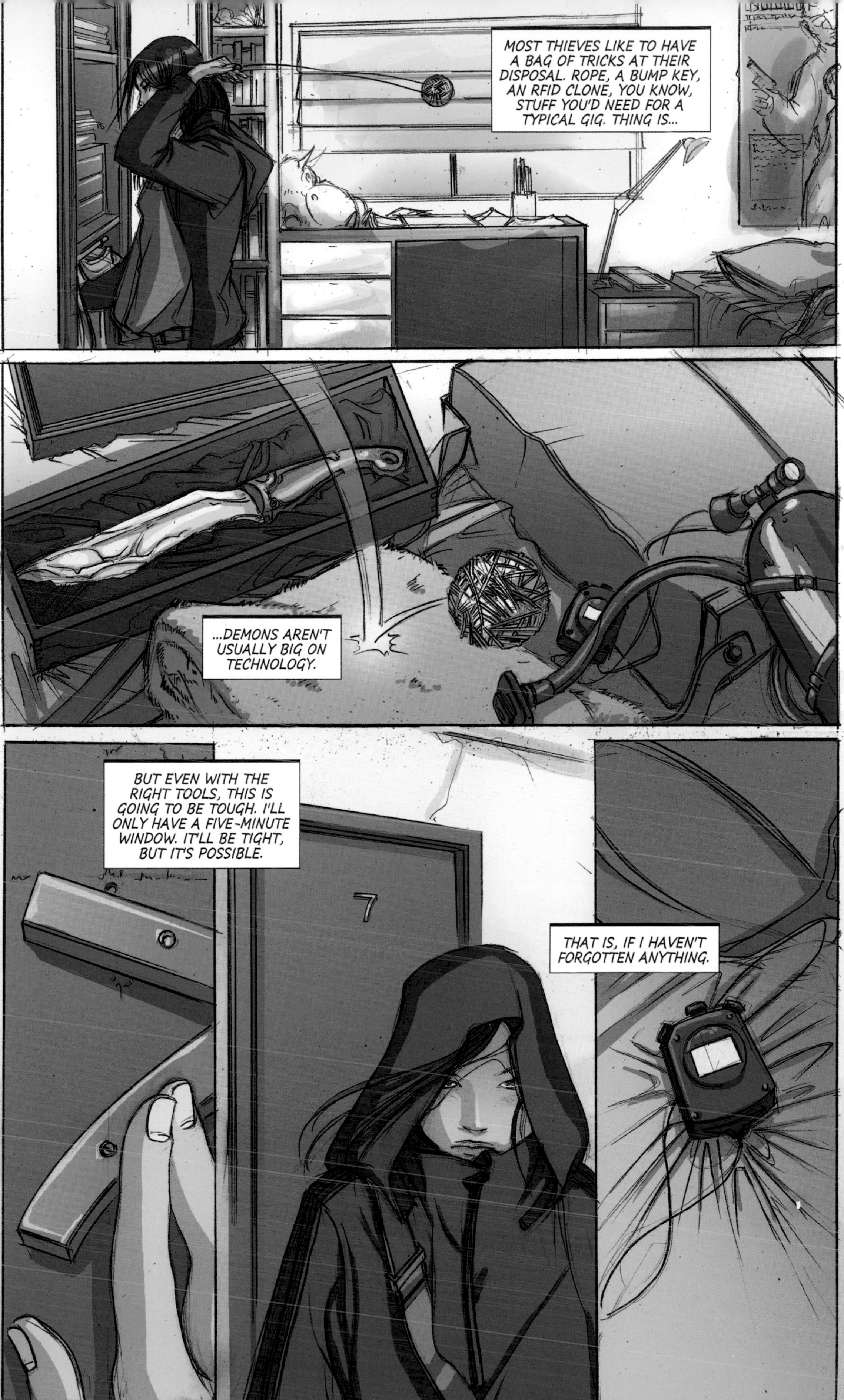
MOST THIEVES LIKE TO HAVE A BAG OF TRICKS AT THEIR DISPOSAL. ROPE, A BUMP KEY, AN RFID CLONE, YOU KNOW, STUFF YOU'D NEED FOR A TYPICAL GIG. THING IS...
...DEMONS AREN'T USUALLY BIG ON TECHNOLOGY.
BUT EVEN WITH THE RIGHT TOOLS, THIS IS GOING TO BE TOUGH. I'LL ONLY HAVE A FIVE-MINUTE WINDOW. IT'LL BE TIGHT, BUT IT'S POSSIBLE.
7
THAT IS, IF I HAVEN'T FORGOTTEN ANYTHING.

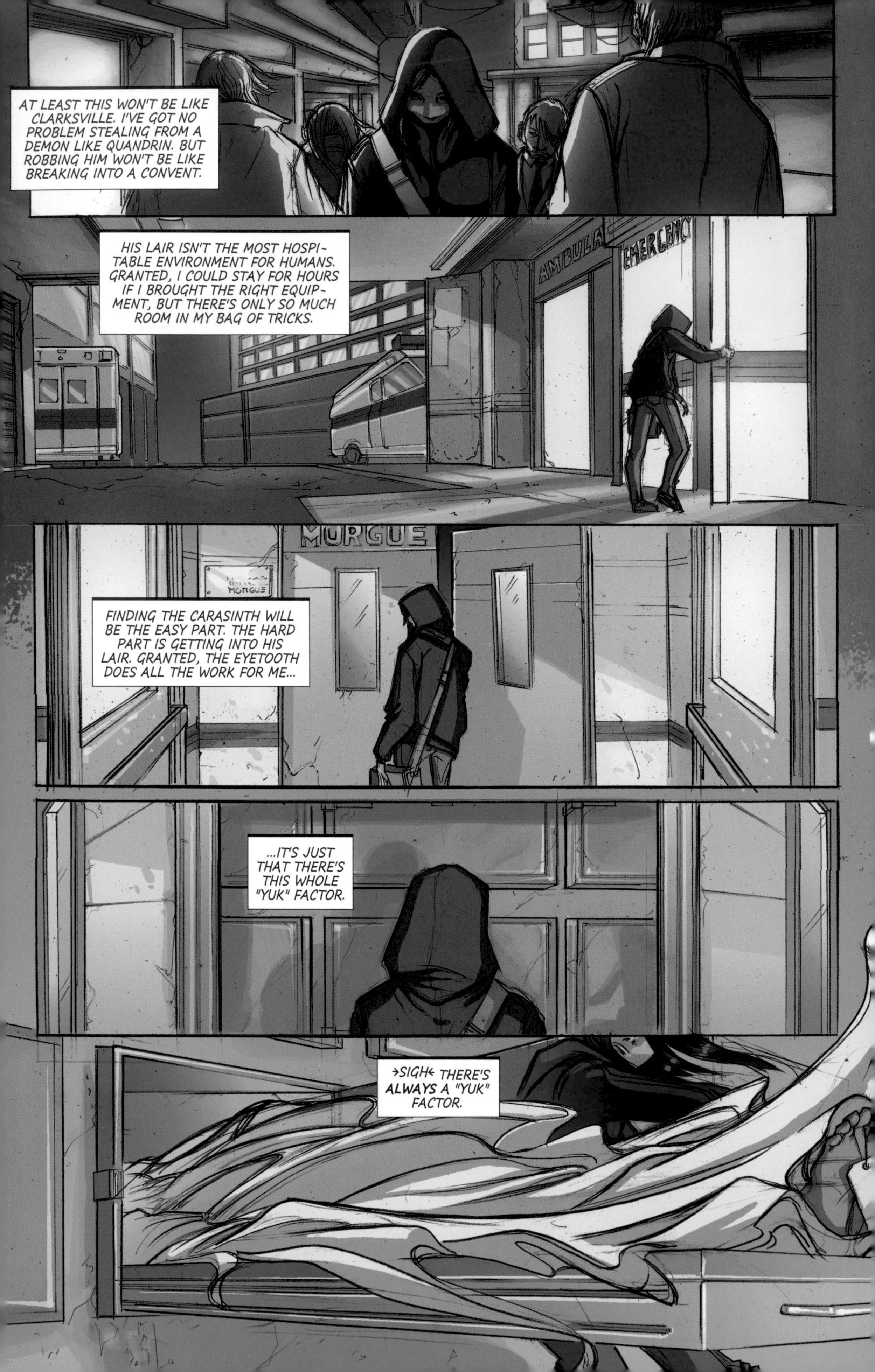
AT LEAST THIS WON'T BE LIKE CLARKSVILLE. I'VE GOT NO PROBLEM STEALING FROM A DEMON LIKE QUANDRIN. BUT ROBBING HIM WON'T BE LIKE BREAKING INTO A CONVENT.
HIS LAIR ISN'T THE MOST HOSPITABLE ENVIRONMENT FOR HUMANS. GRANTED, I COULD STAY FOR HOURS IF I BROUGHT THE RIGHT EQUIPMENT, BUT THERE'S ONLY SO MUCH ROOM IN MY BAG OF TRICKS.
AMBULA
EMERGENCY
MORGUE
MORGUE
FINDING THE CARASINTH WILL BE THE EASY PART. THE HARD PART IS GETTING INTO HIS LAIR. GRANTED, THE EYETOOTH DOES ALL THE WORK FOR ME...
...IT'S JUST THAT THERE'S THIS WHOLE "YUK" FACTOR.
→SIGH← THERE'S **ALWAYS** A "YUK" FACTOR.

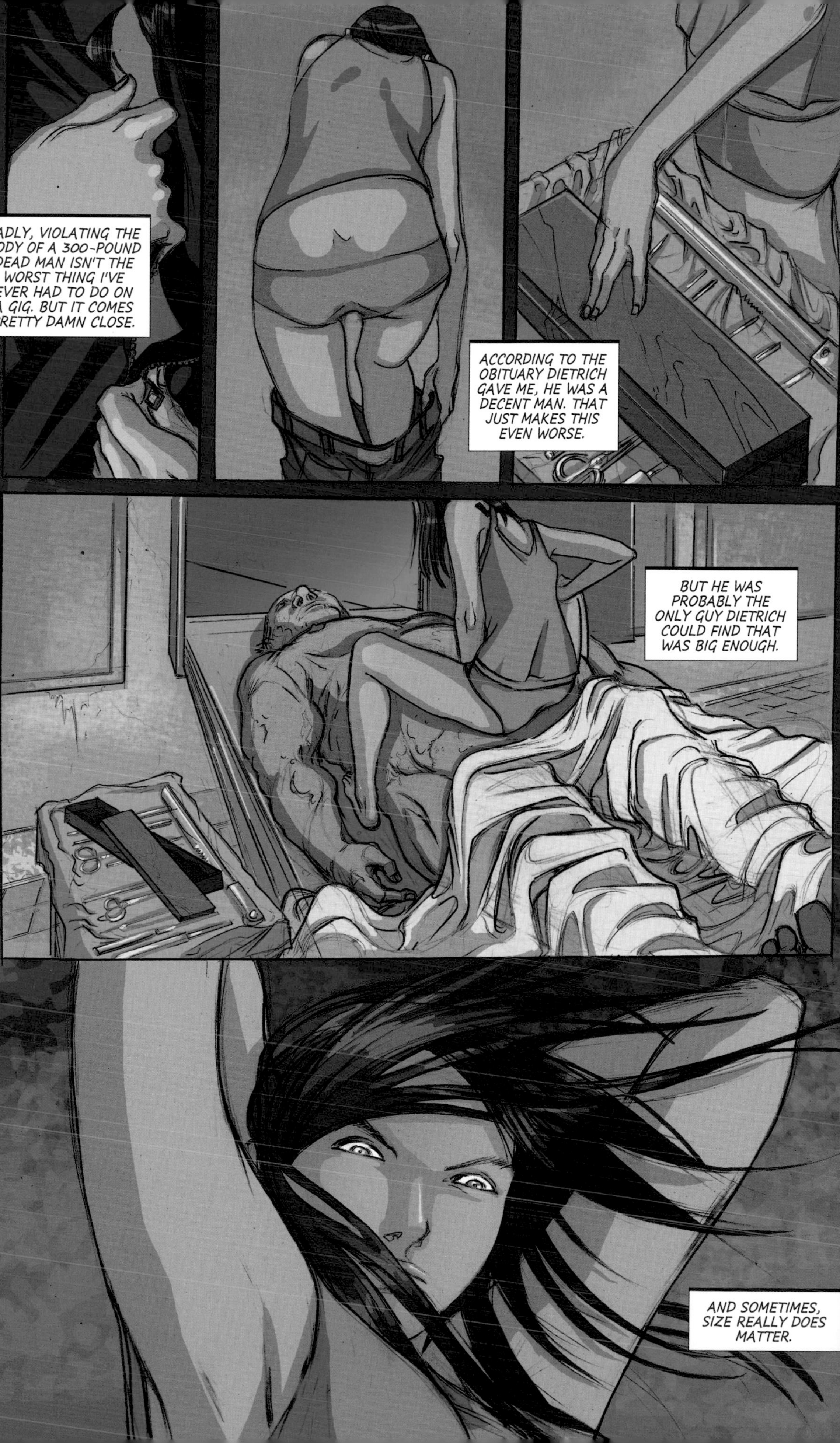
SADLY, VIOLATING THE BODY OF A 300-POUND DEAD MAN ISN'T THE WORST THING I'VE EVER HAD TO DO ON A GIG. BUT IT COMES PRETTY DAMN CLOSE.
ACCORDING TO THE OBITUARY DIETRICH GAVE ME, HE WAS A DECENT MAN. THAT JUST MAKES THIS EVEN WORSE.
BUT HE WAS PROBABLY THE ONLY GUY DIETRICH COULD FIND THAT WAS BIG ENOUGH.
AND SOMETIMES, SIZE REALLY DOES MATTER.

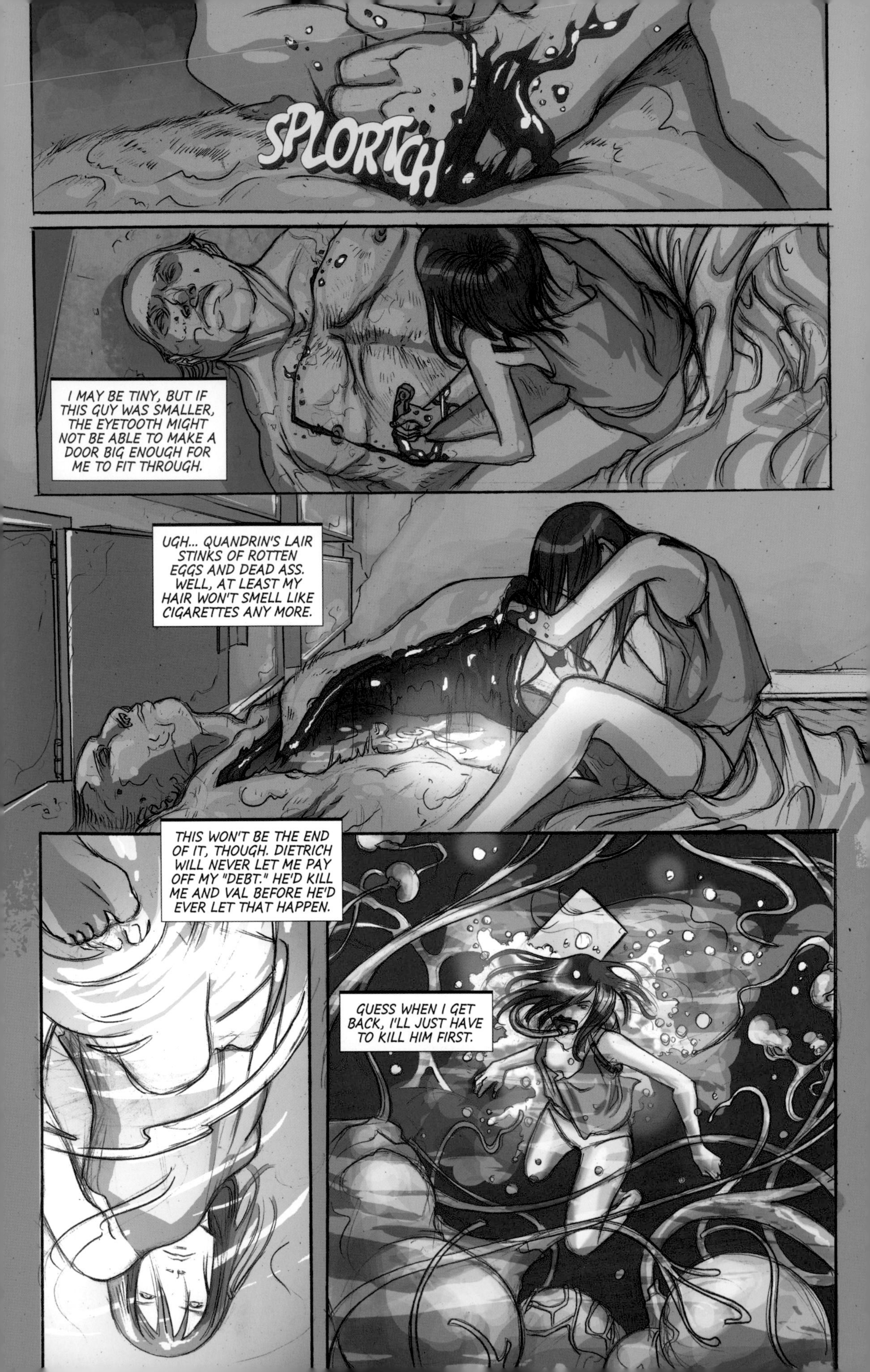
SPLORTCH
I MAY BE TINY, BUT IF THIS GUY WAS SMALLER, THE EYETOOTH MIGHT NOT BE ABLE TO MAKE A DOOR BIG ENOUGH FOR ME TO FIT THROUGH.
UGH... QUANDRIN'S LAIR STINKS OF ROTTEN EGGS AND DEAD ASS. WELL, AT LEAST MY HAIR WON'T SMELL LIKE CIGARETTES ANY MORE.
THIS WON'T BE THE END OF IT, THOUGH. DIETRICH WILL NEVER LET ME PAY OFF MY "DEBT." HE'D KILL ME AND VAL BEFORE HE'D EVER LET THAT HAPPEN.
GUESS WHEN I GET BACK, I'LL JUST HAVE TO KILL HIM FIRST.

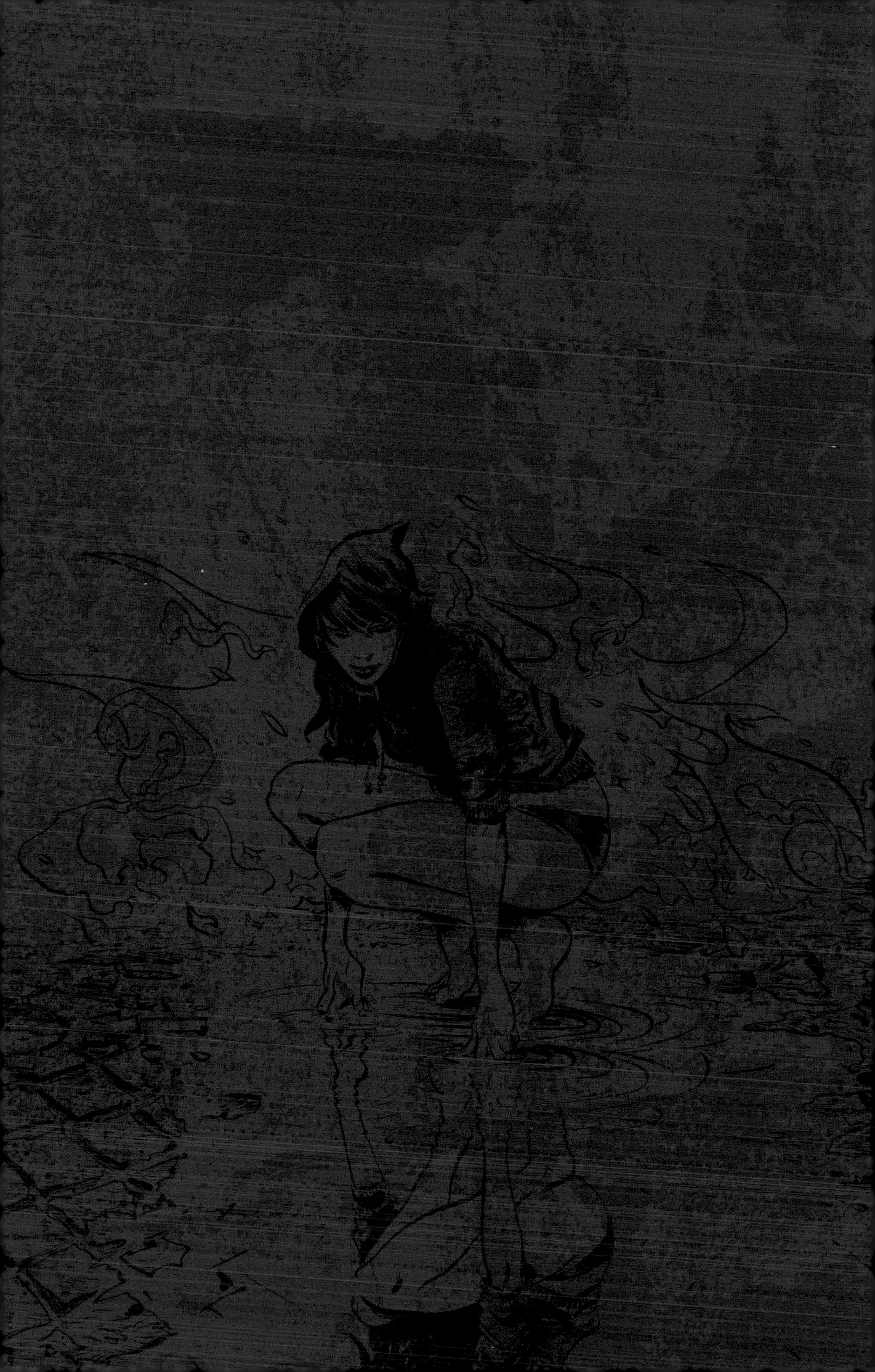

CHAPTER II

Wherein Lucifer faces unemployment and receives an unexpected wake-up call.

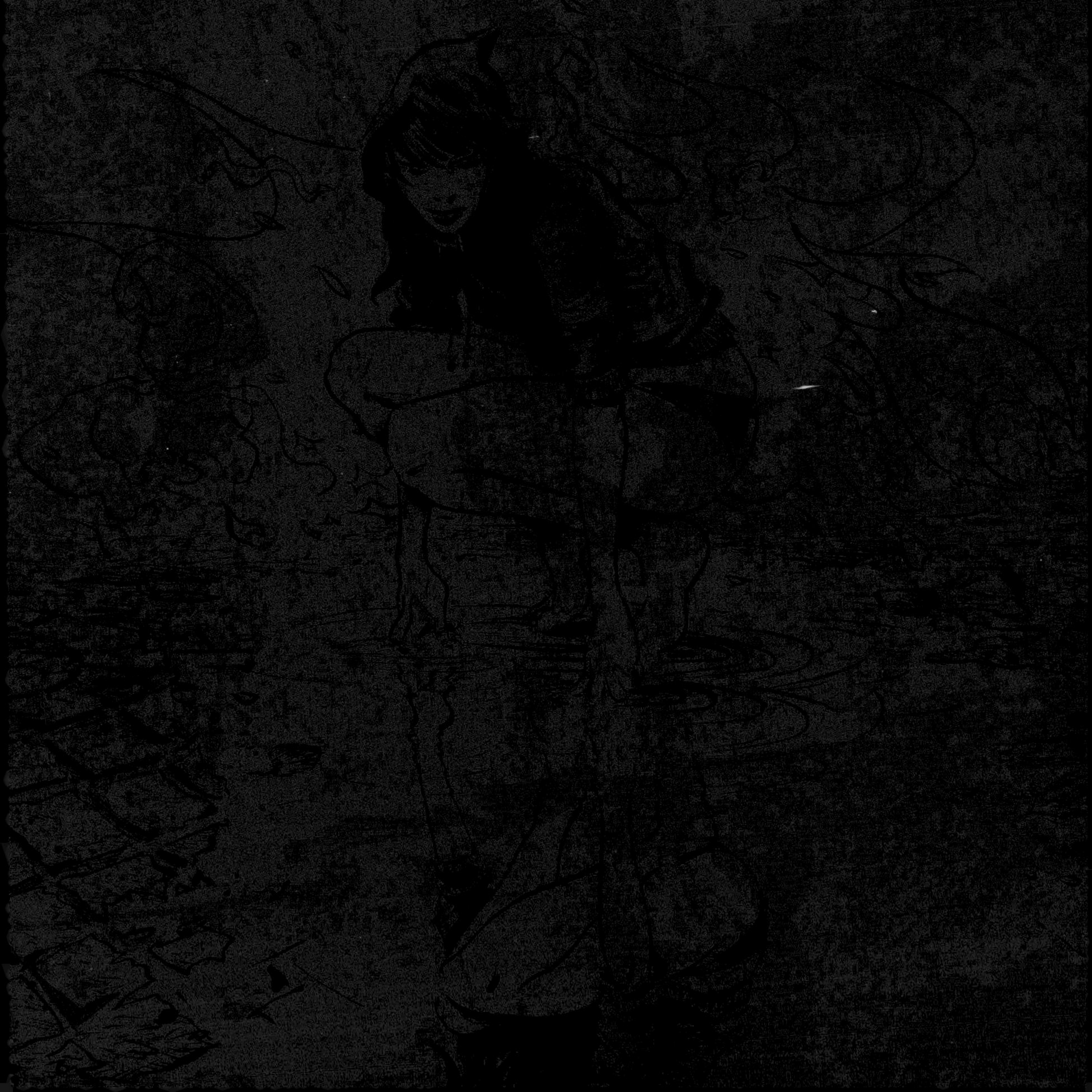

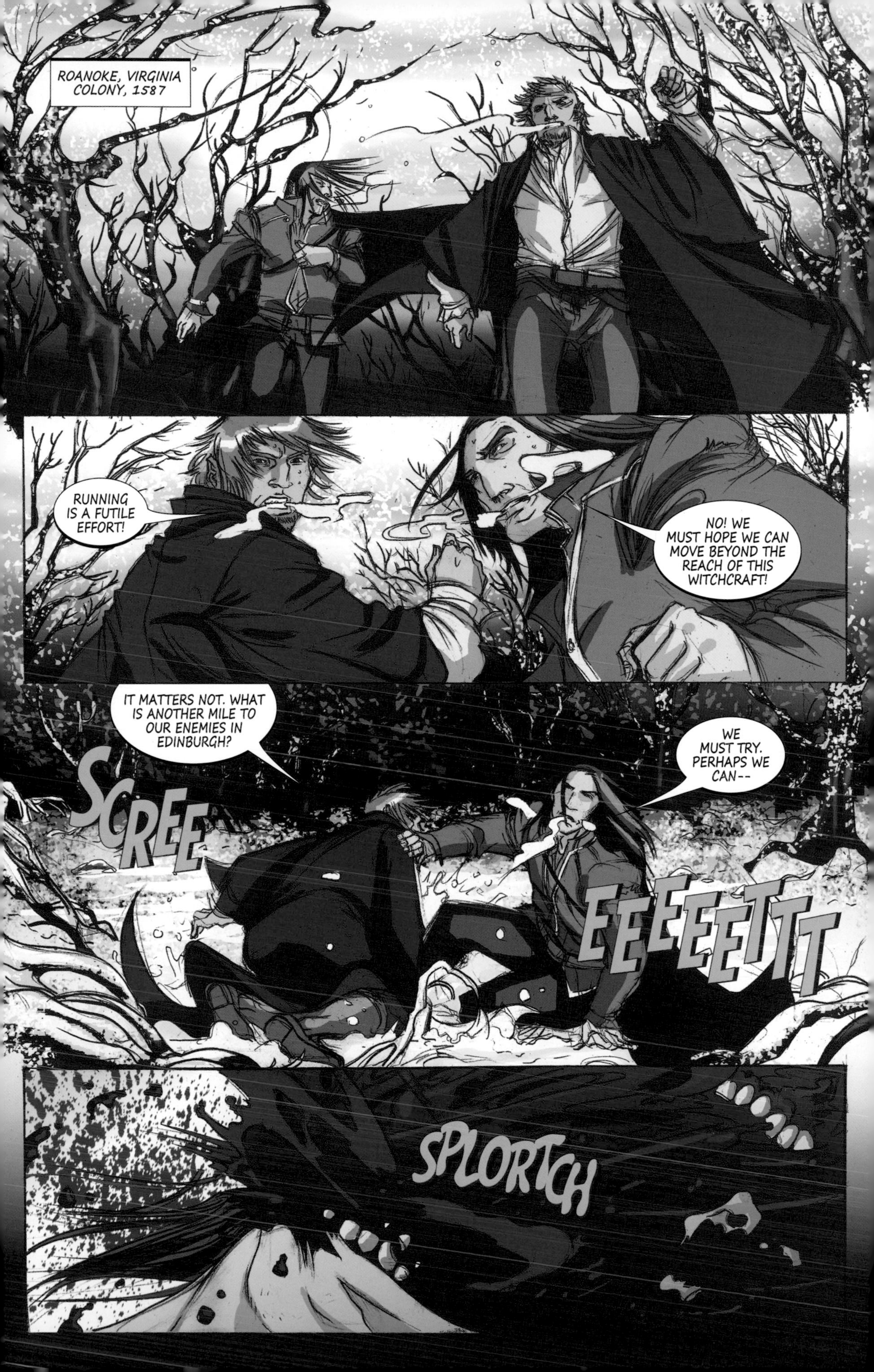
ROANOKE, VIRGINIA COLONY, 1587
RUNNING IS A FUTILE EFFORT!
NO! WE MUST HOPE WE CAN MOVE BEYOND THE REACH OF THIS WITCHCRAFT!
IT MATTERS NOT. WHAT IS ANOTHER MILE TO OUR ENEMIES IN EDINBURGH?
WE MUST TRY. PERHAPS WE CAN--
SCREE
EEEEETTT
SPLORTCH

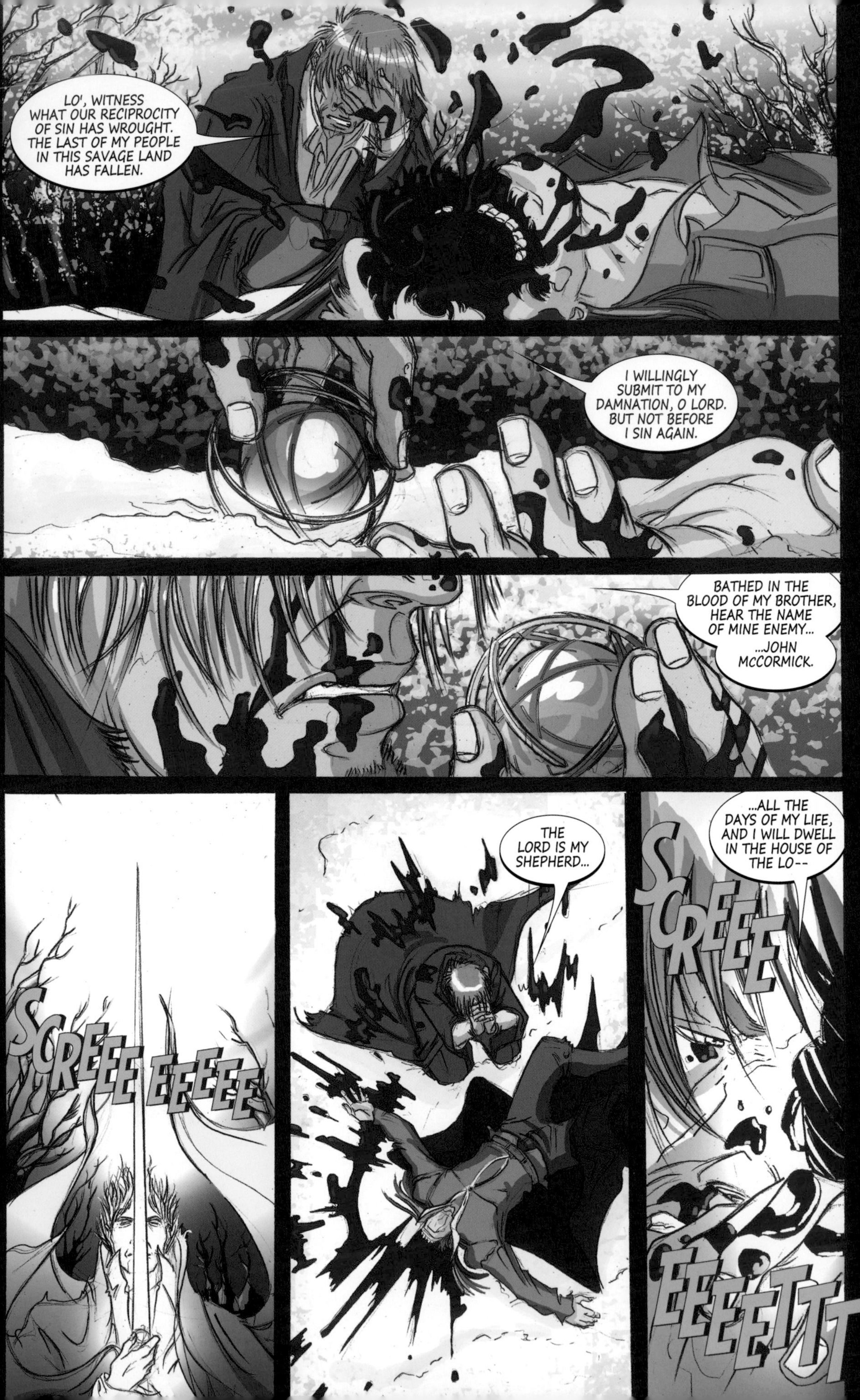
LO', WITNESS WHAT OUR RECIPROCITY OF SIN HAS WROUGHT. THE LAST OF MY PEOPLE IN THIS SAVAGE LAND HAS FALLEN.
I WILLINGLY SUBMIT TO MY DAMNATION, O LORD. BUT NOT BEFORE I SIN AGAIN.
BATHED IN THE BLOOD OF MY BROTHER, HEAR THE NAME OF MINE ENEMY...
...JOHN McCORMICK.
SCREEE EEEEEE
THE LORD IS MY SHEPHERD...
...ALL THE DAYS OF MY LIFE, AND I WILL DWELL IN THE HOUSE OF THE LO--
SCREEE
EEEEETTT

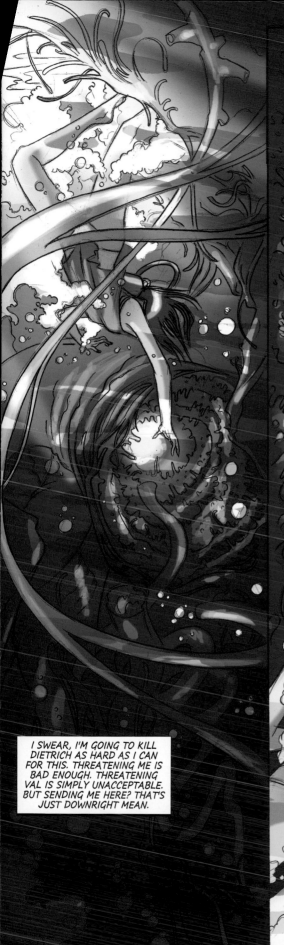

I SWEAR, I'M GOING TO KILL DIETRICH AS HARD AS I CAN FOR THIS. THREATENING ME IS BAD ENOUGH. THREATENING VAL IS SIMPLY UNACCEPTABLE. BUT SENDING ME HERE? THAT'S JUST DOWNRIGHT MEAN.

AND WHATEVER THIS FOUL LIQUID IS, ITS STENCH IS BLEEDING THROUGH THE REBREATHER.

PLUS, IT KINDA STINGS.

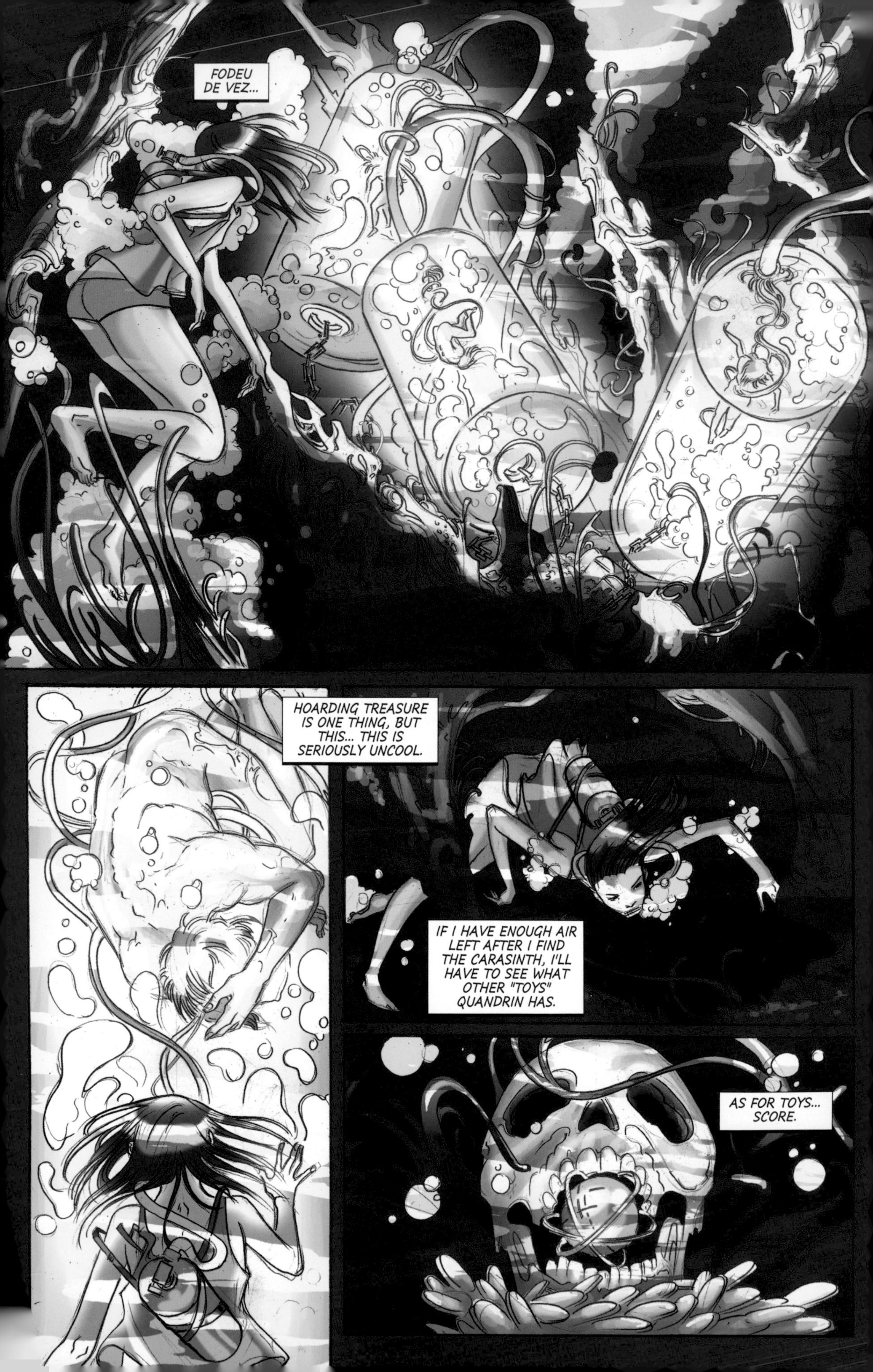
FODEU DE VEZ...
HOARDING TREASURE IS ONE THING, BUT THIS... THIS IS SERIOUSLY UNCOOL.
IF I HAVE ENOUGH AIR LEFT AFTER I FIND THE CARASINTH, I'LL HAVE TO SEE WHAT OTHER "TOYS" QUANDRIN HAS.
AS FOR TOYS... SCORE.

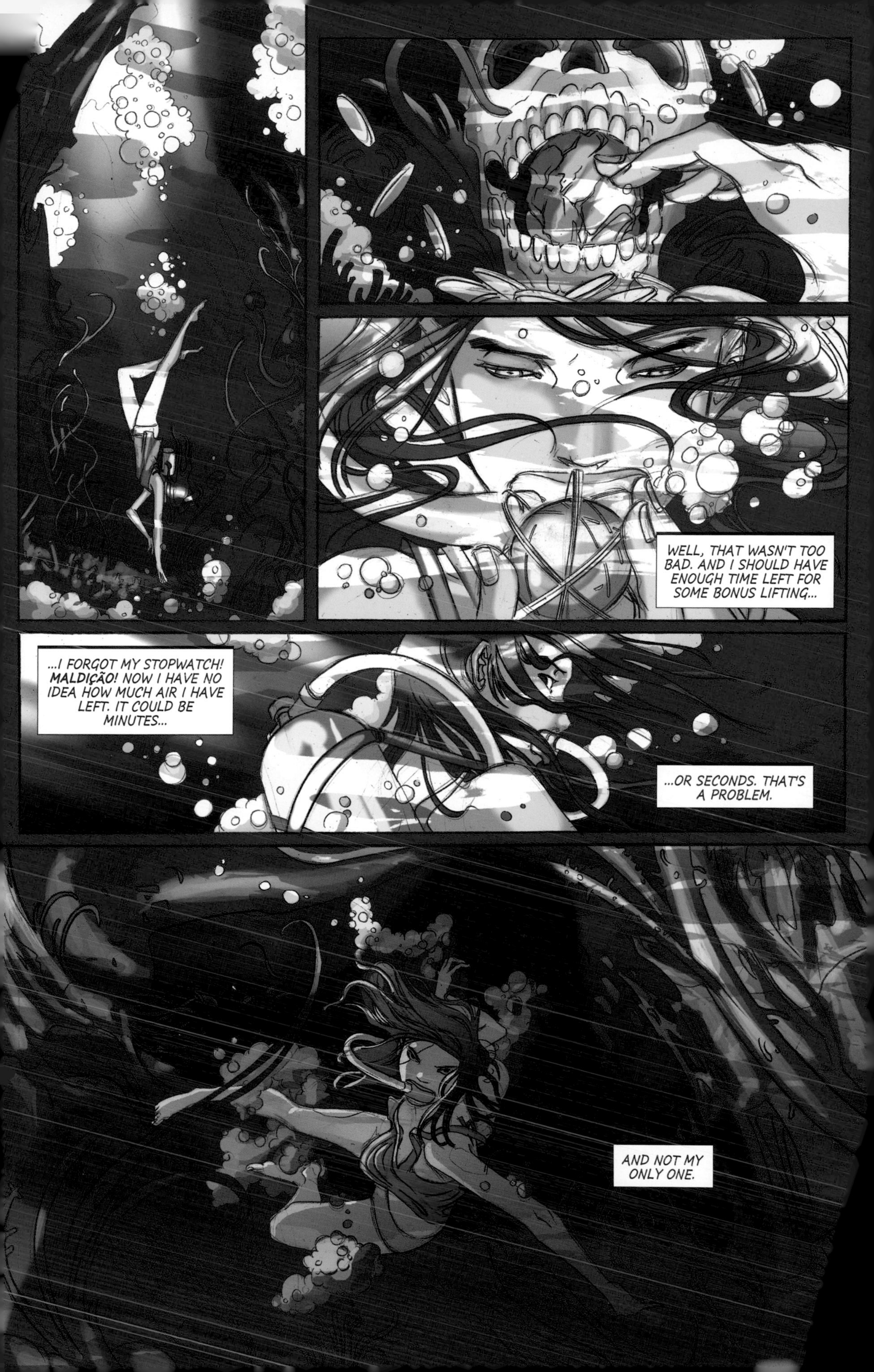
WELL, THAT WASN'T TOO BAD. AND I SHOULD HAVE ENOUGH TIME LEFT FOR SOME BONUS LIFTING...
...I FORGOT MY STOPWATCH! MALDIÇÃO! NOW I HAVE NO IDEA HOW MUCH AIR I HAVE LEFT. IT COULD BE MINUTES...
...OR SECONDS. THAT'S A PROBLEM.
AND NOT MY ONLY ONE.

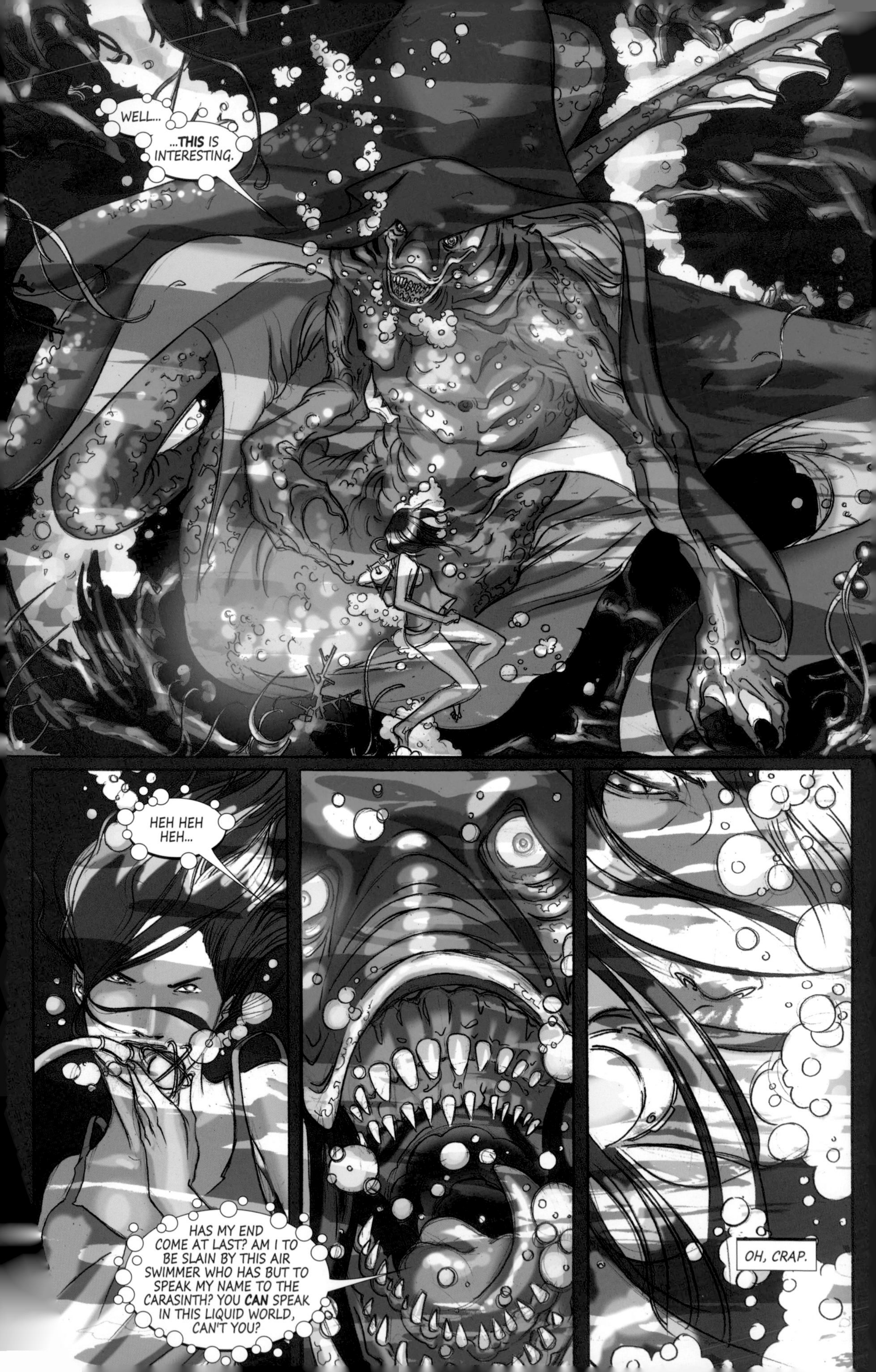
WELL...
...THIS IS INTERESTING.
HEH HEH HEH...
HAS MY END COME AT LAST? AM I TO BE SLAIN BY THIS AIR SWIMMER WHO HAS BUT TO SPEAK MY NAME TO THE CARASINTH? YOU CAN SPEAK IN THIS LIQUID WORLD, CAN'T YOU?
OH, CRAP.

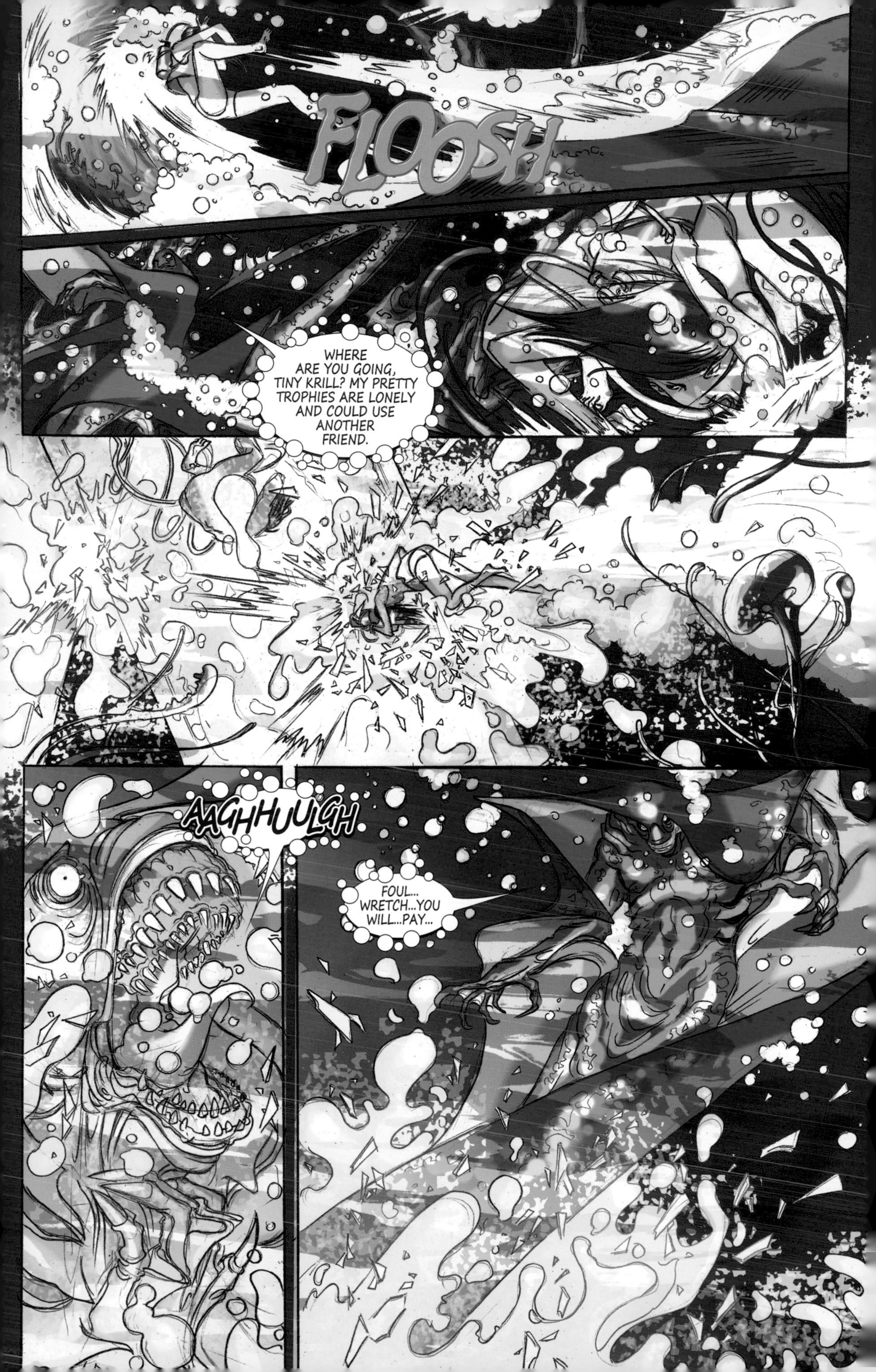
FLOOSH
WHERE ARE YOU GOING, TINY KRILL? MY PRETTY TROPHIES ARE LONELY AND COULD USE ANOTHER FRIEND.
AAGHHUULGH
FOUL... WRETCH...YOU WILL...PAY...

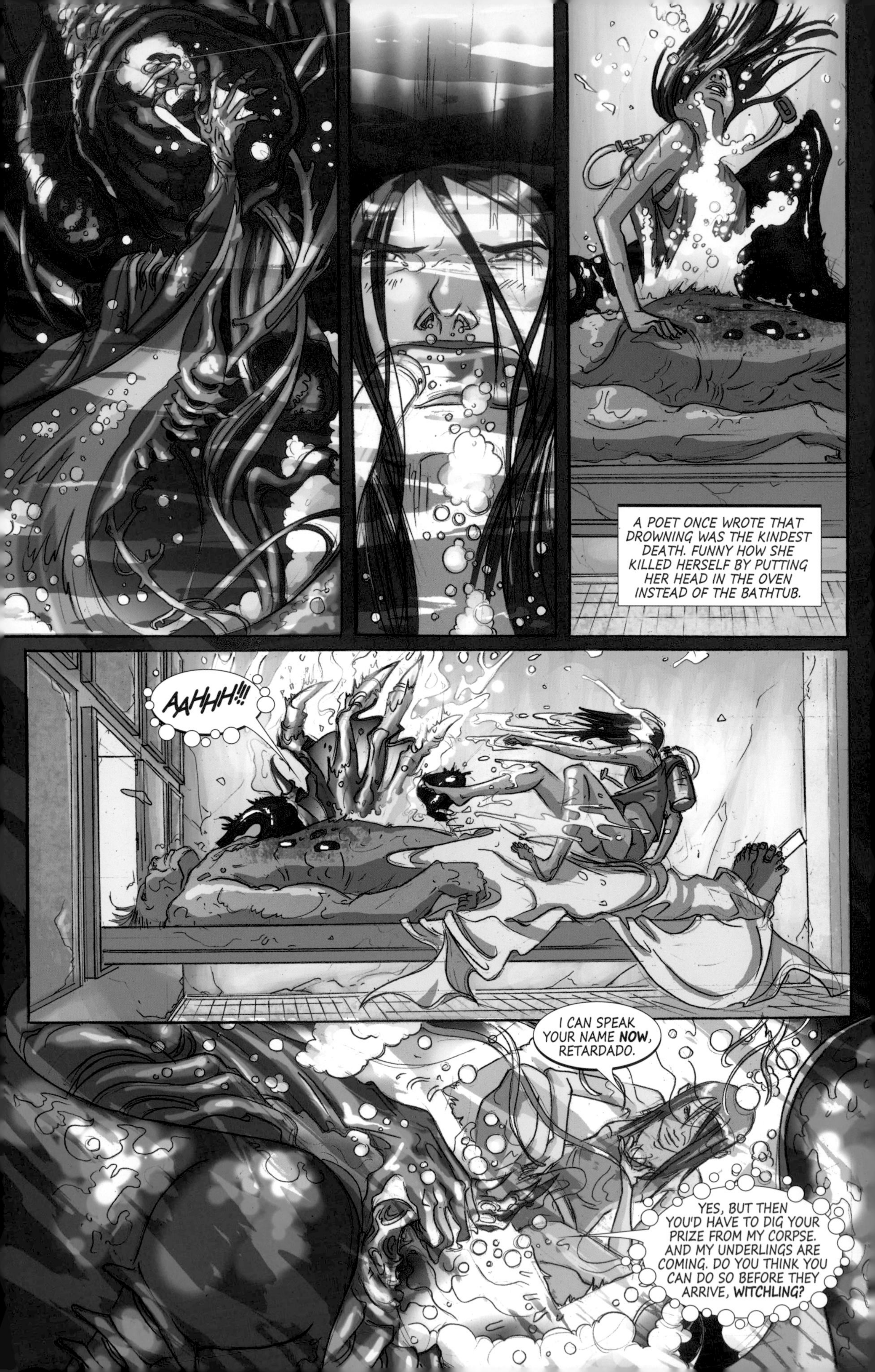
A POET ONCE WROTE THAT DROWNING WAS THE KINDEST DEATH. FUNNY HOW SHE KILLED HERSELF BY PUTTING HER HEAD IN THE OVEN INSTEAD OF THE BATHTUB.
AAHHH!!!
I CAN SPEAK YOUR NAME NOW, RETARDADO.
YES, BUT THEN YOU'D HAVE TO DIG YOUR PRIZE FROM MY CORPSE. AND MY UNDERLINGS ARE COMING. DO YOU THINK YOU CAN DO SO BEFORE THEY ARRIVE, WITCHLING?

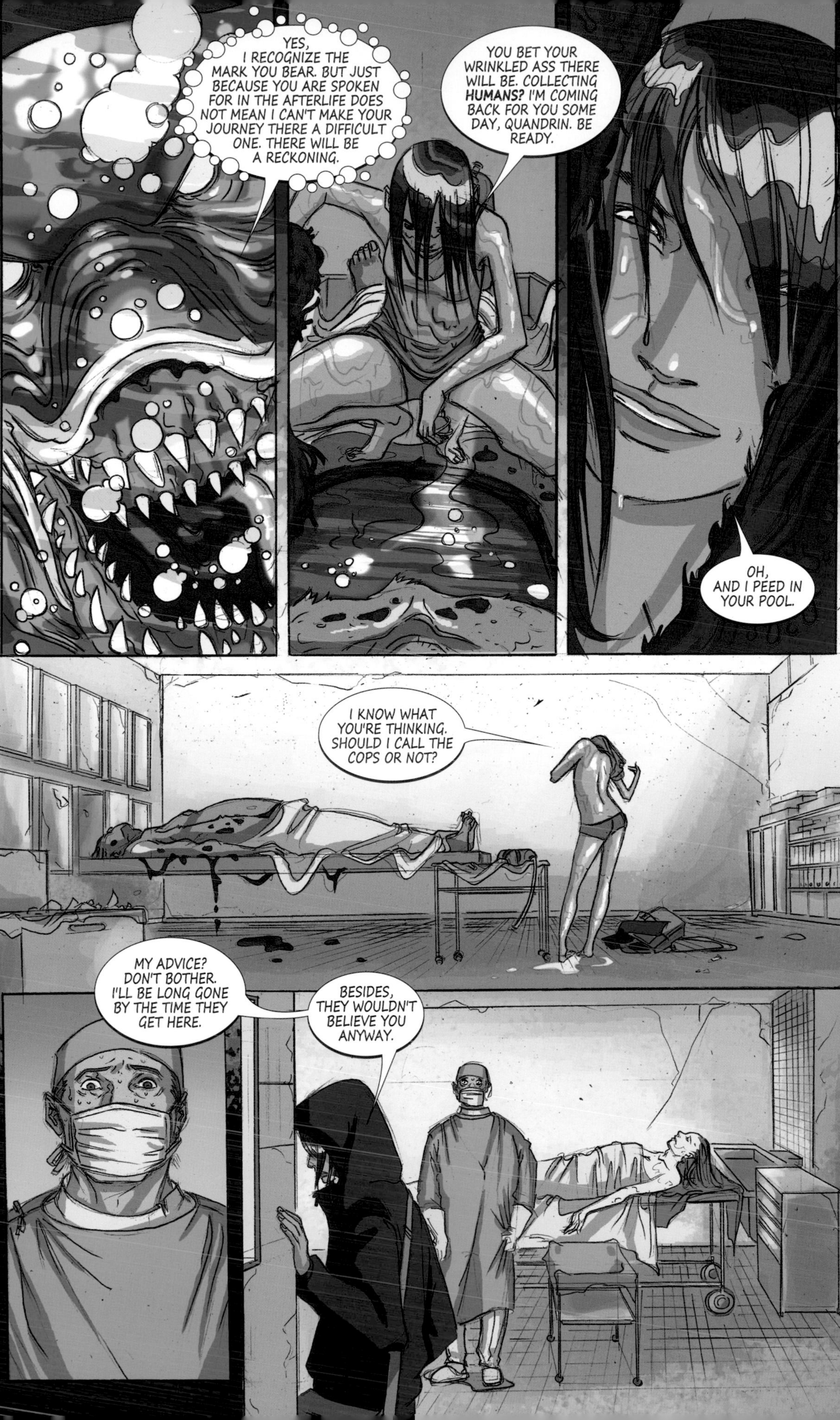
YES, I RECOGNIZE THE MARK YOU BEAR. BUT JUST BECAUSE YOU ARE SPOKEN FOR IN THE AFTERLIFE DOES NOT MEAN I CAN'T MAKE YOUR JOURNEY THERE A DIFFICULT ONE. THERE WILL BE A RECKONING.
YOU BET YOUR WRINKLED ASS THERE WILL BE. COLLECTING HUMANS? I'M COMING BACK FOR YOU SOME DAY, QUANDRIN. BE READY.
OH, AND I PEED IN YOUR POOL.
I KNOW WHAT YOU'RE THINKING. SHOULD I CALL THE COPS OR NOT?
MY ADVICE? DON'T BOTHER. I'LL BE LONG GONE BY THE TIME THEY GET HERE.
BESIDES, THEY WOULDN'T BELIEVE YOU ANYWAY.

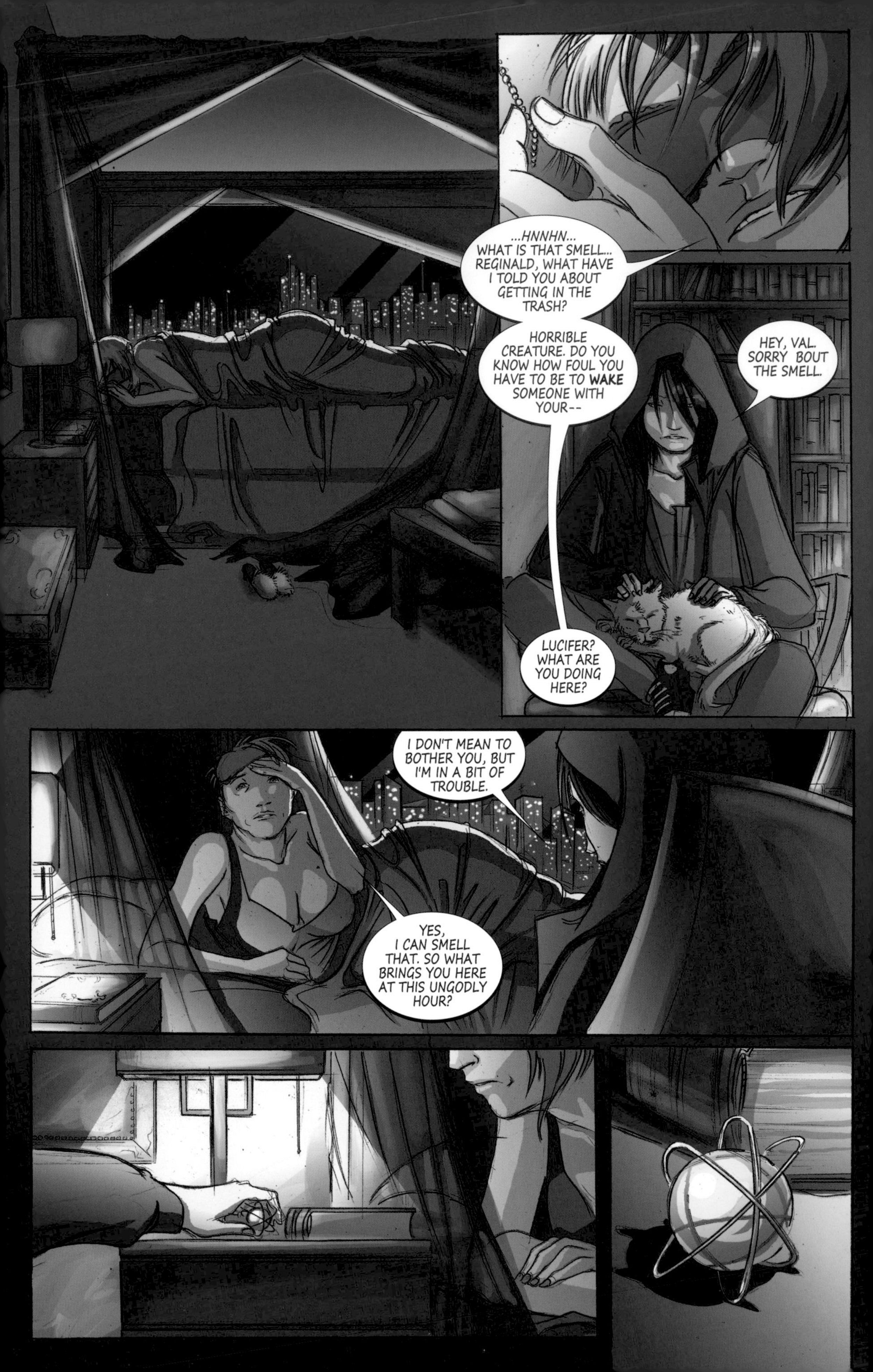
...HNNHN... WHAT IS THAT SMELL... REGINALD, WHAT HAVE I TOLD YOU ABOUT GETTING IN THE TRASH?
HORRIBLE CREATURE. DO YOU KNOW HOW FOUL YOU HAVE TO BE TO **WAKE** SOMEONE WITH YOUR--
HEY, VAL. SORRY BOUT THE SMELL.
LUCIFER? WHAT ARE YOU DOING HERE?
I DON'T MEAN TO BOTHER YOU, BUT I'M IN A BIT OF TROUBLE.
YES, I CAN SMELL THAT. SO WHAT BRINGS YOU HERE AT THIS UNGODLY HOUR?

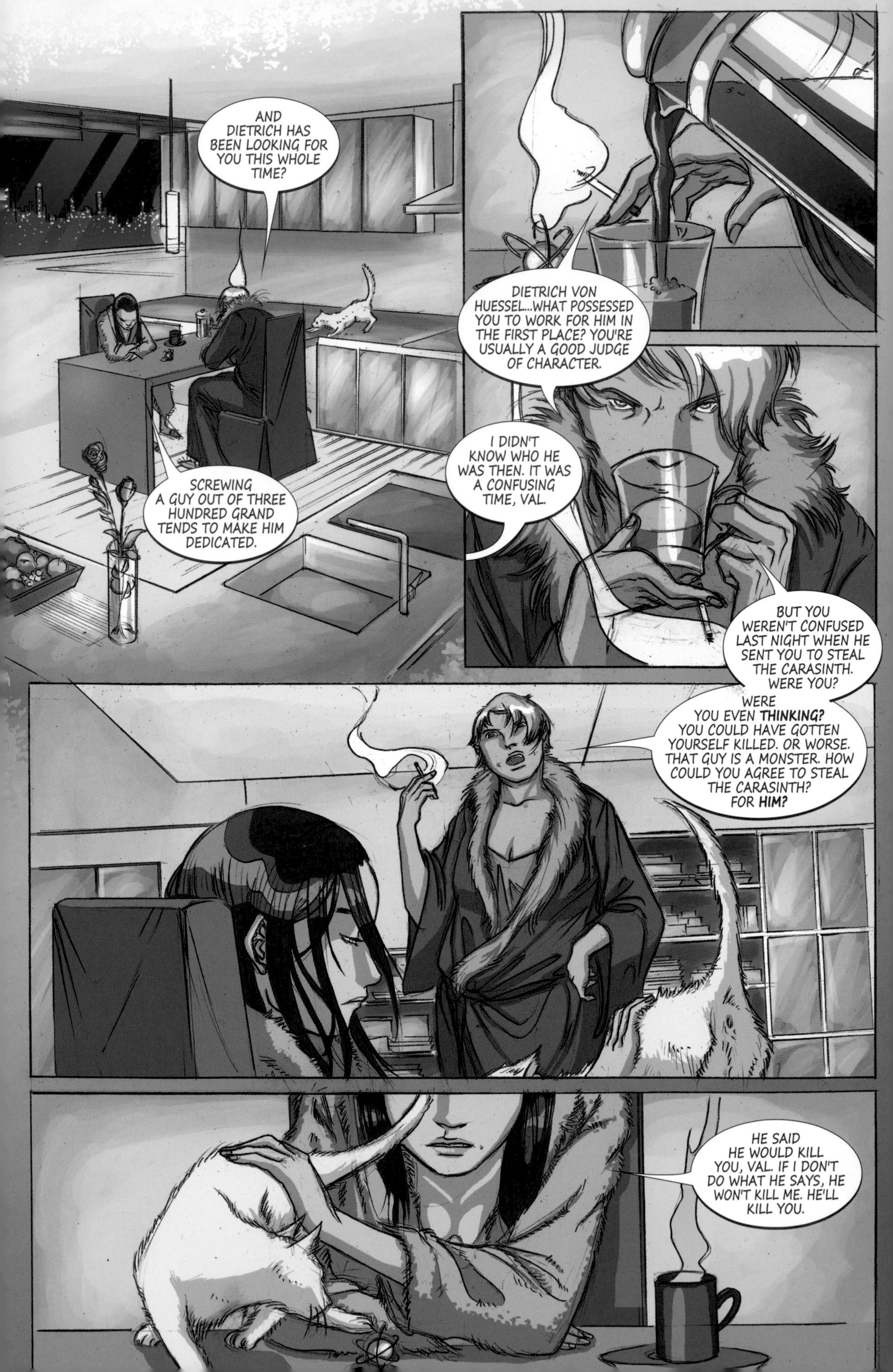
AND DIETRICH HAS BEEN LOOKING FOR YOU THIS WHOLE TIME?
SCREWING A GUY OUT OF THREE HUNDRED GRAND TENDS TO MAKE HIM DEDICATED.
DIETRICH VON HUESSEL...WHAT POSSESSED YOU TO WORK FOR HIM IN THE FIRST PLACE? YOU'RE USUALLY A GOOD JUDGE OF CHARACTER.
I DIDN'T KNOW WHO HE WAS THEN. IT WAS A CONFUSING TIME, VAL.
BUT YOU WEREN'T CONFUSED LAST NIGHT WHEN HE SENT YOU TO STEAL THE CARASINTH. WERE YOU?
WERE YOU EVEN **THINKING?** YOU COULD HAVE GOTTEN YOURSELF KILLED. OR WORSE. THAT GUY IS A MONSTER. HOW COULD YOU AGREE TO STEAL THE CARASINTH? FOR **HIM?**
HE SAID HE WOULD KILL YOU, VAL. IF I DON'T DO WHAT HE SAYS, HE WON'T KILL ME. HE'LL KILL YOU.

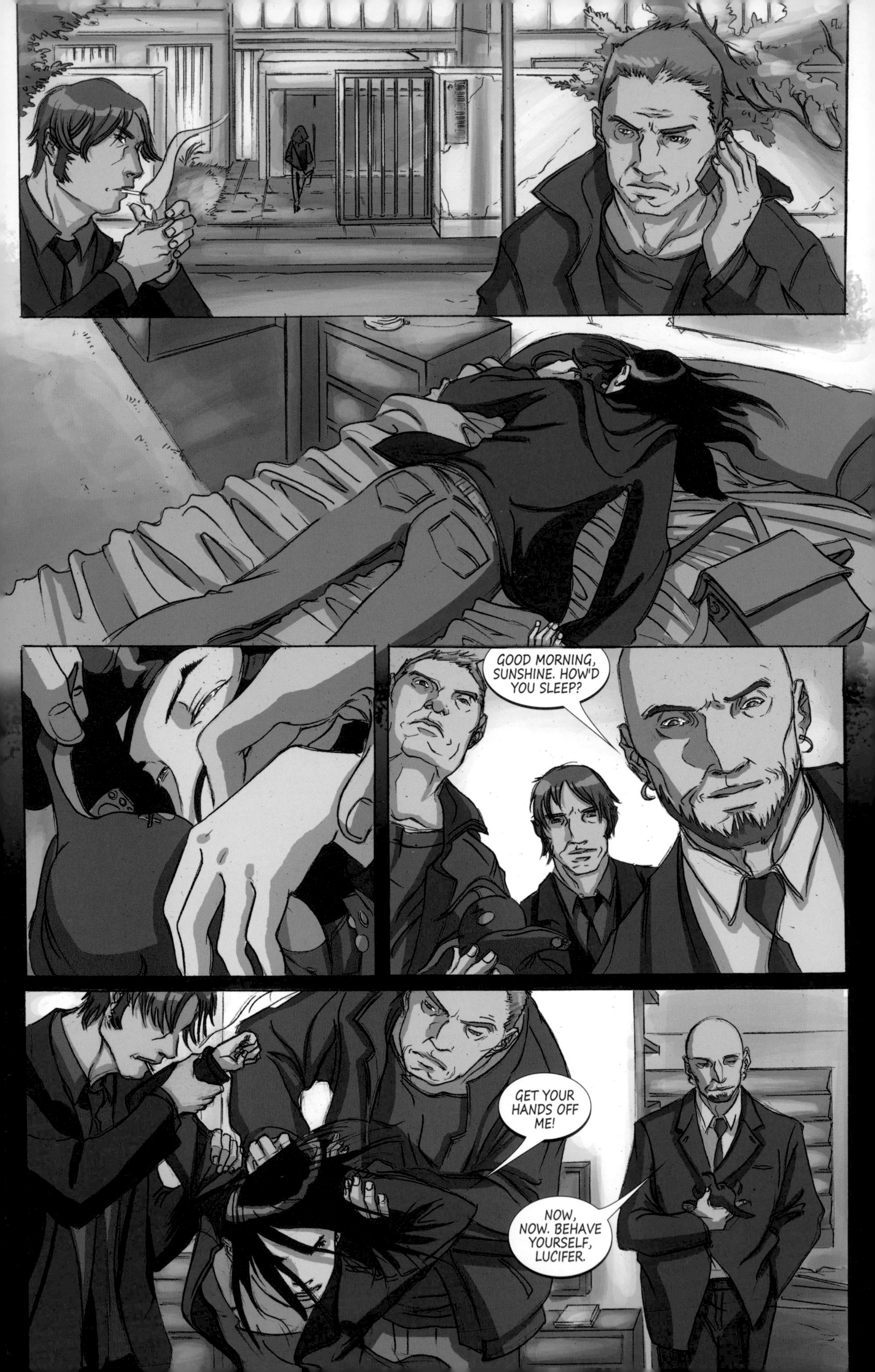
GOOD MORNING, SUNSHINE. HOW'D YOU SLEEP?
GET YOUR HANDS OFF ME!
NOW, NOW. BEHAVE YOURSELF, LUCIFER.

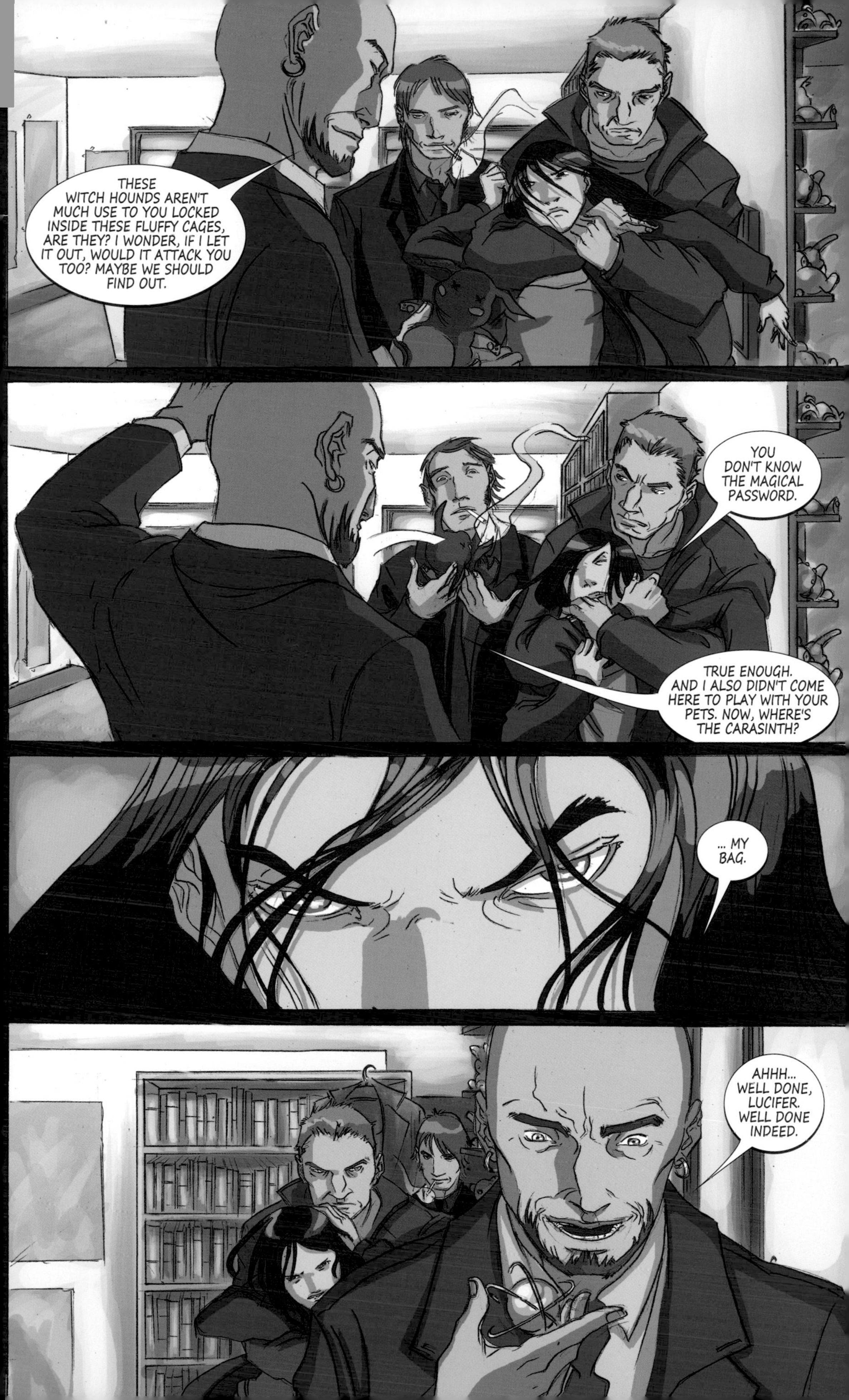
THESE WITCH HOUNDS AREN'T MUCH USE TO YOU LOCKED INSIDE THESE FLUFFY CAGES, ARE THEY? I WONDER, IF I LET IT OUT, WOULD IT ATTACK YOU TOO? MAYBE WE SHOULD FIND OUT.
YOU DON'T KNOW THE MAGICAL PASSWORD.
TRUE ENOUGH. AND I ALSO DIDN'T COME HERE TO PLAY WITH YOUR PETS. NOW, WHERE'S THE CARASINTH?
... MY BAG.
AHHH... WELL DONE, LUCIFER. WELL DONE INDEED.

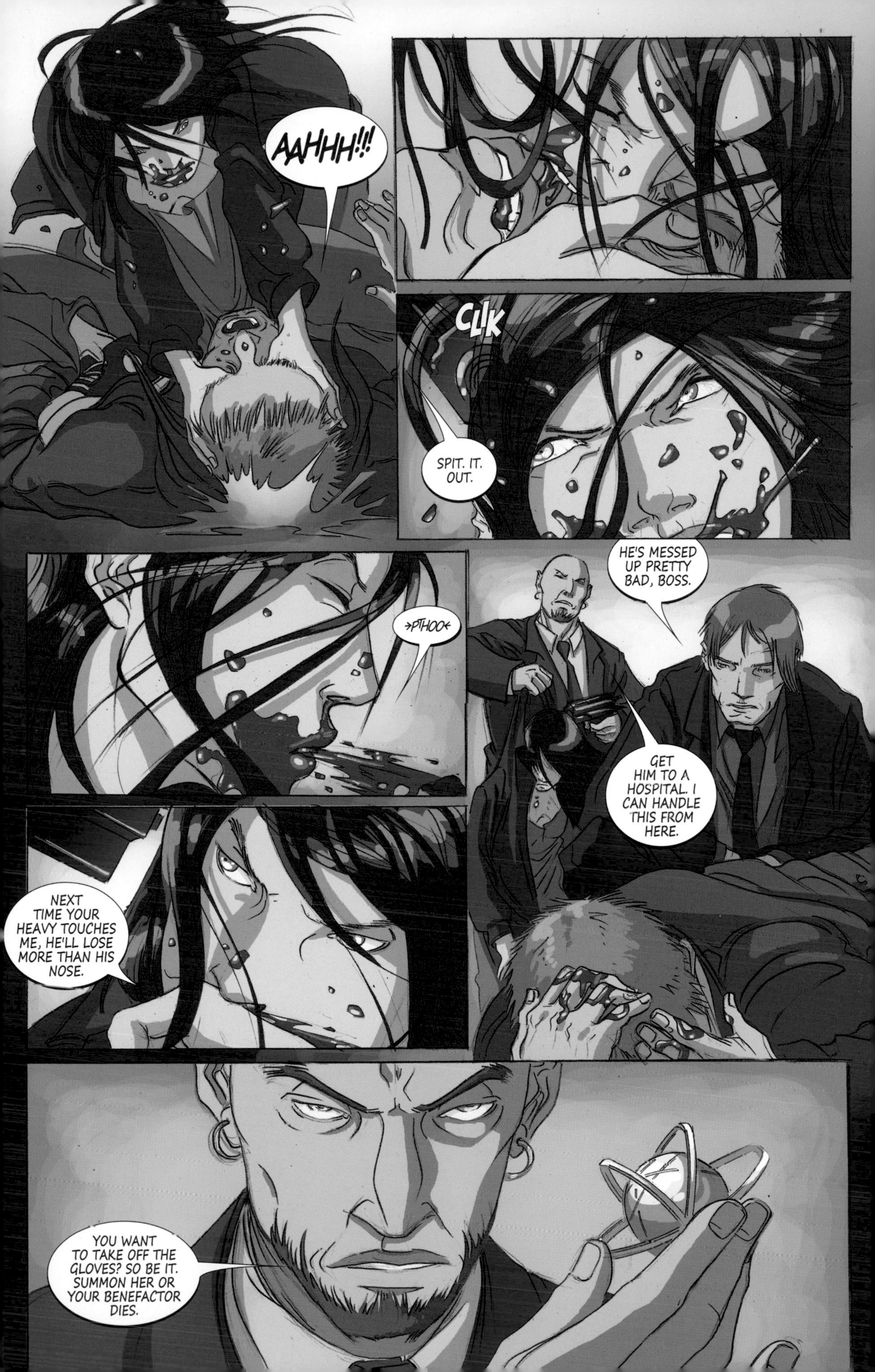
AAHHH!!!
CLIK
SPIT. IT. OUT.
>PTHOO<
HE'S MESSED UP PRETTY BAD, BOSS.
GET HIM TO A HOSPITAL. I CAN HANDLE THIS FROM HERE.
NEXT TIME YOUR HEAVY TOUCHES ME, HE'LL LOSE MORE THAN HIS NOSE.
YOU WANT TO TAKE OFF THE GLOVES? SO BE IT. SUMMON HER OR YOUR BENEFACTOR DIES.

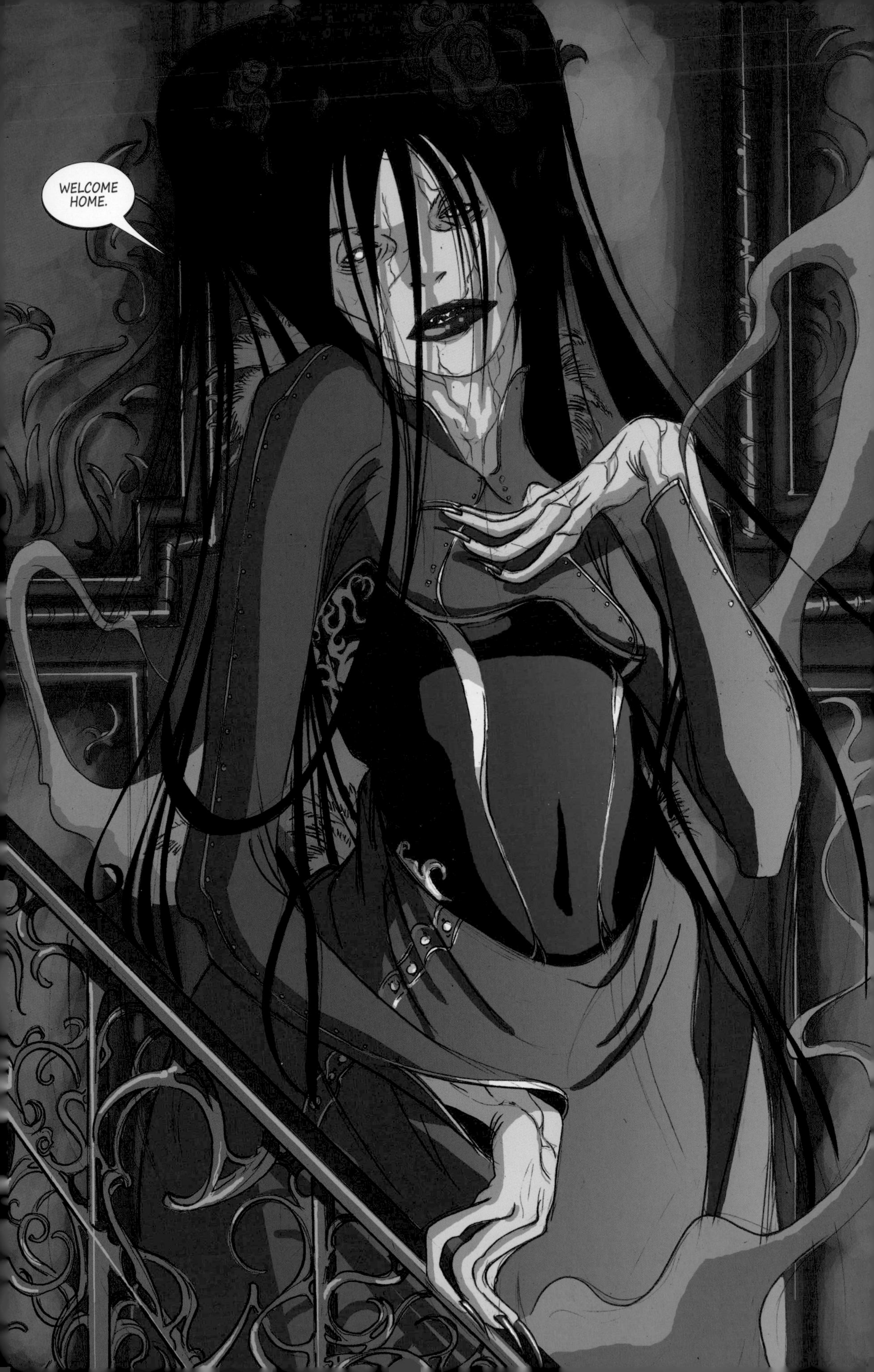
WELCOME HOME.

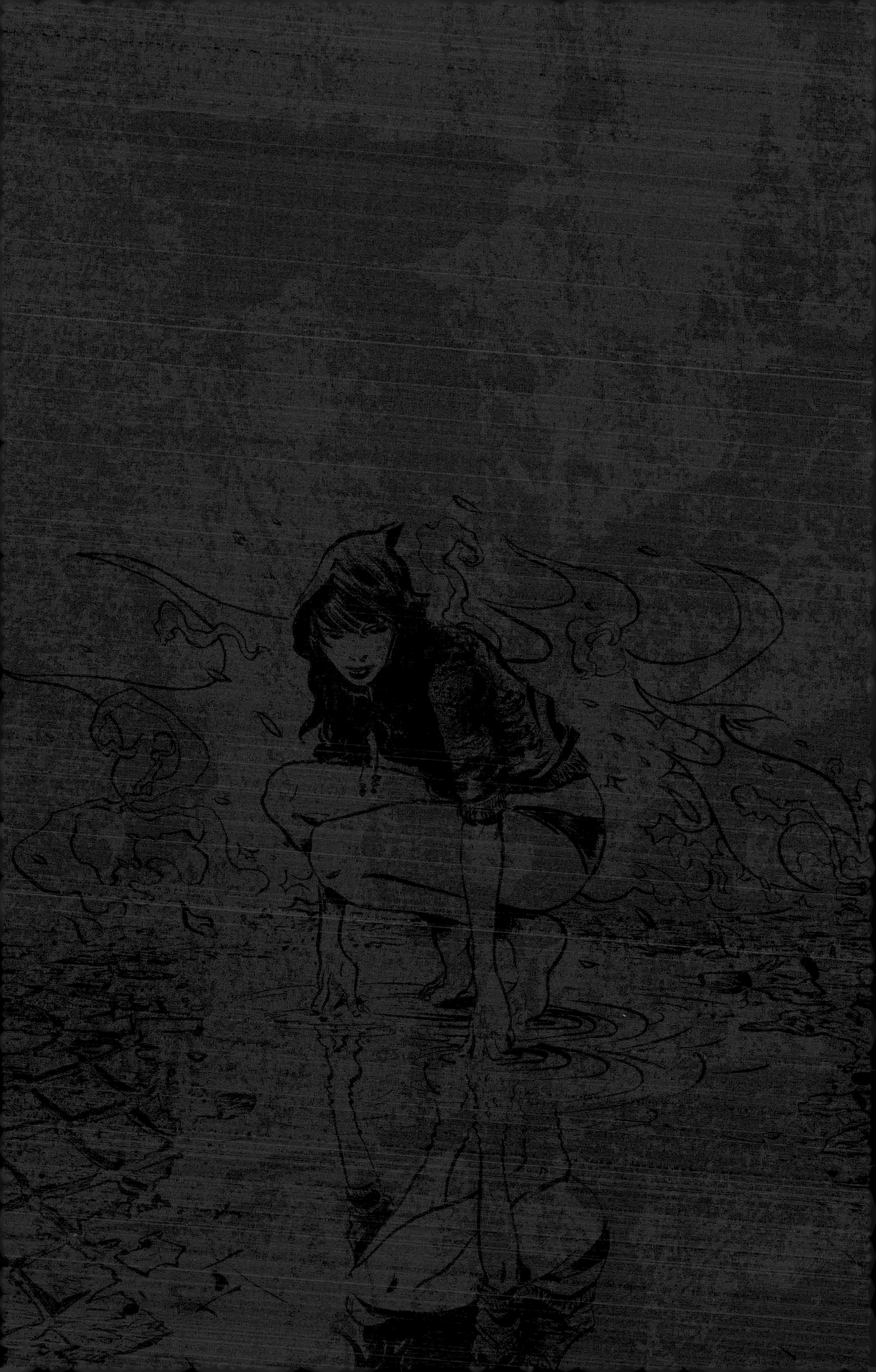

CHAPTER III

Wherein Lucifer learns to drive, gets her picture taken, and calls in a favor from a Peeping Tom.

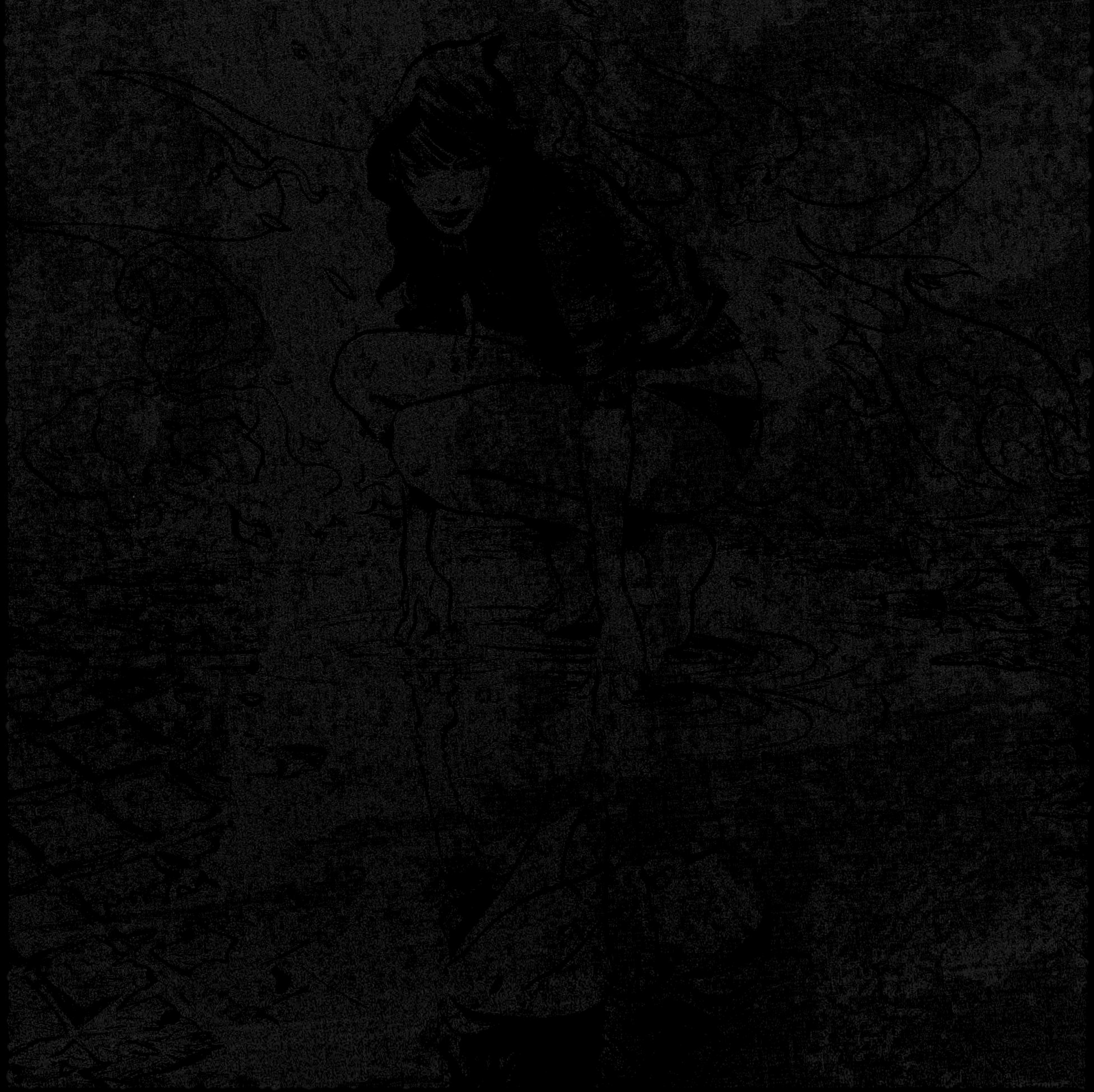

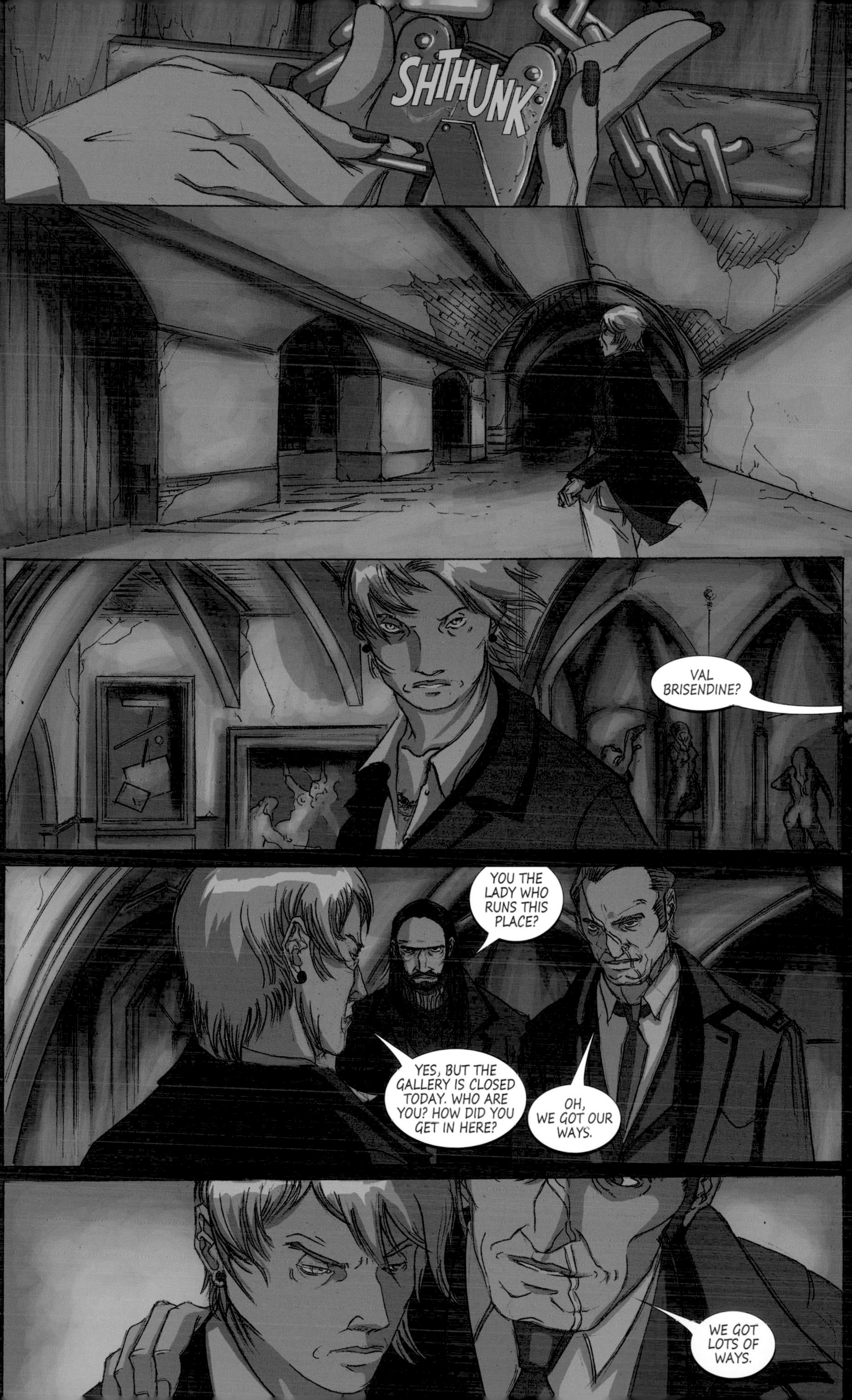
SHITHUNK
VAL BRISENDINE?
YOU THE LADY WHO RUNS THIS PLACE?
YES, BUT THE GALLERY IS CLOSED TODAY. WHO ARE YOU? HOW DID YOU GET IN HERE?
OH, WE GOT OUR WAYS.
WE GOT LOTS OF WAYS.

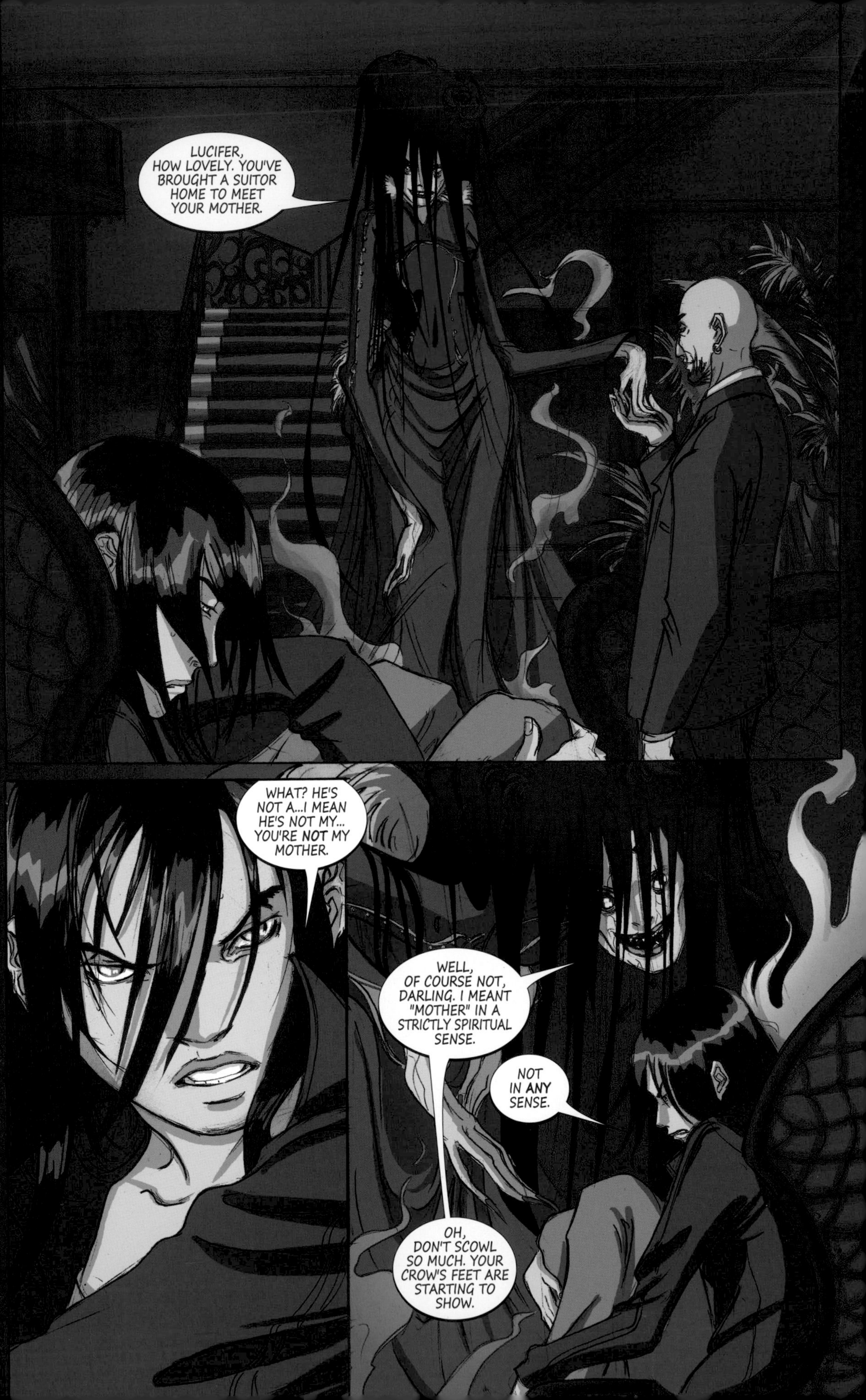
LUCIFER, HOW LOVELY. YOU'VE BROUGHT A SUITOR HOME TO MEET YOUR MOTHER.
WHAT? HE'S NOT A...I MEAN HE'S NOT MY... YOU'RE **NOT** MY MOTHER.
WELL, OF COURSE NOT, DARLING. I MEANT "MOTHER" IN A STRICTLY SPIRITUAL SENSE.
NOT IN **ANY** SENSE.
OH, DON'T SCOWL SO MUCH. YOUR CROW'S FEET ARE STARTING TO SHOW.

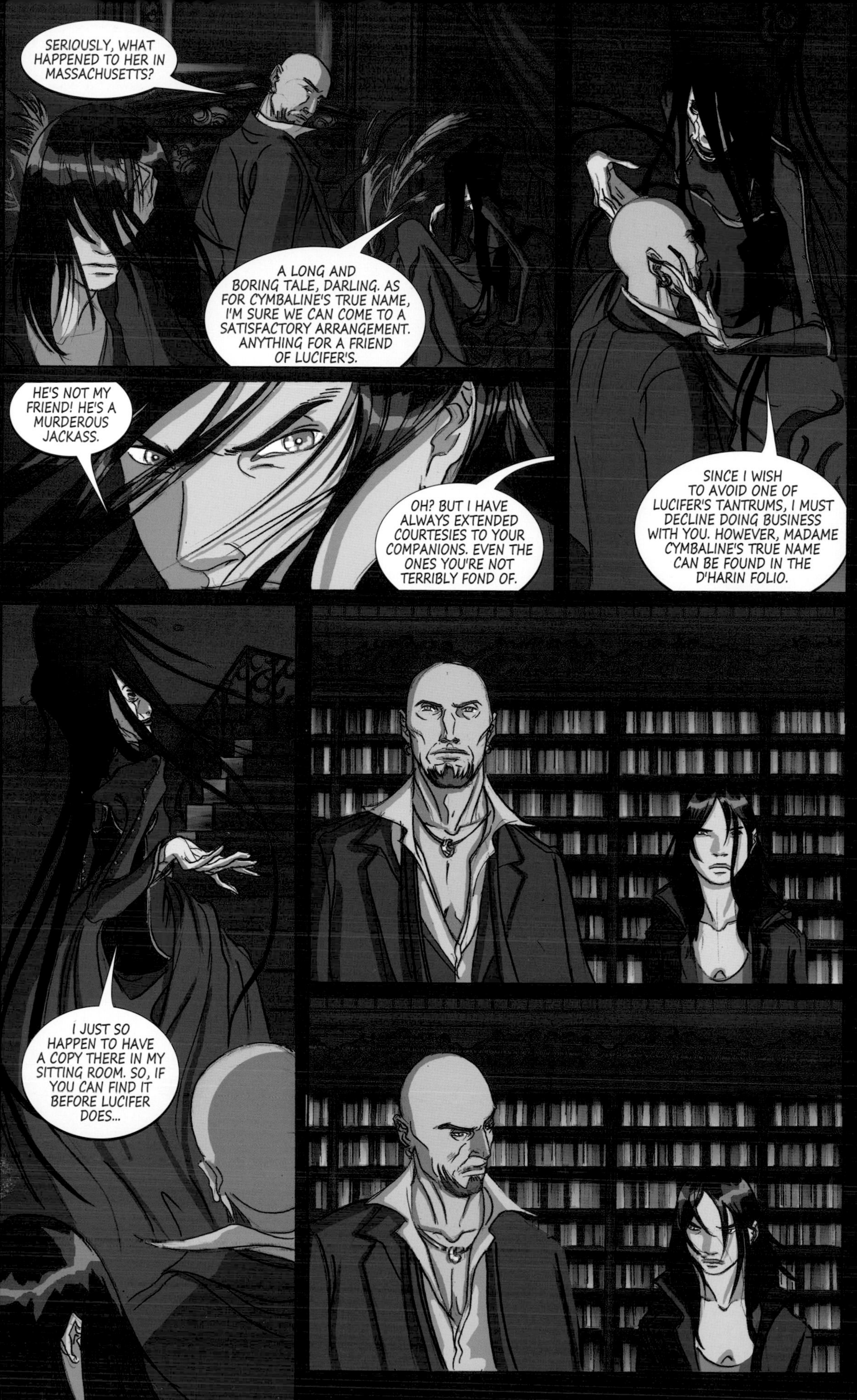
SERIOUSLY, WHAT HAPPENED TO HER IN MASSACHUSETTS?
A LONG AND BORING TALE, DARLING. AS FOR CYMBALINE'S TRUE NAME, I'M SURE WE CAN COME TO A SATISFACTORY ARRANGEMENT. ANYTHING FOR A FRIEND OF LUCIFER'S.
HE'S NOT MY FRIEND! HE'S A MURDEROUS JACKASS.
OH? BUT I HAVE ALWAYS EXTENDED COURTESIES TO YOUR COMPANIONS. EVEN THE ONES YOU'RE NOT TERRIBLY FOND OF.
SINCE I WISH TO AVOID ONE OF LUCIFER'S TANTRUMS, I MUST DECLINE DOING BUSINESS WITH YOU. HOWEVER, MADAME CYMBALINE'S TRUE NAME CAN BE FOUND IN THE D'HARIN FOLIO.
I JUST SO HAPPEN TO HAVE A COPY THERE IN MY SITTING ROOM. SO, IF YOU CAN FIND IT BEFORE LUCIFER DOES...

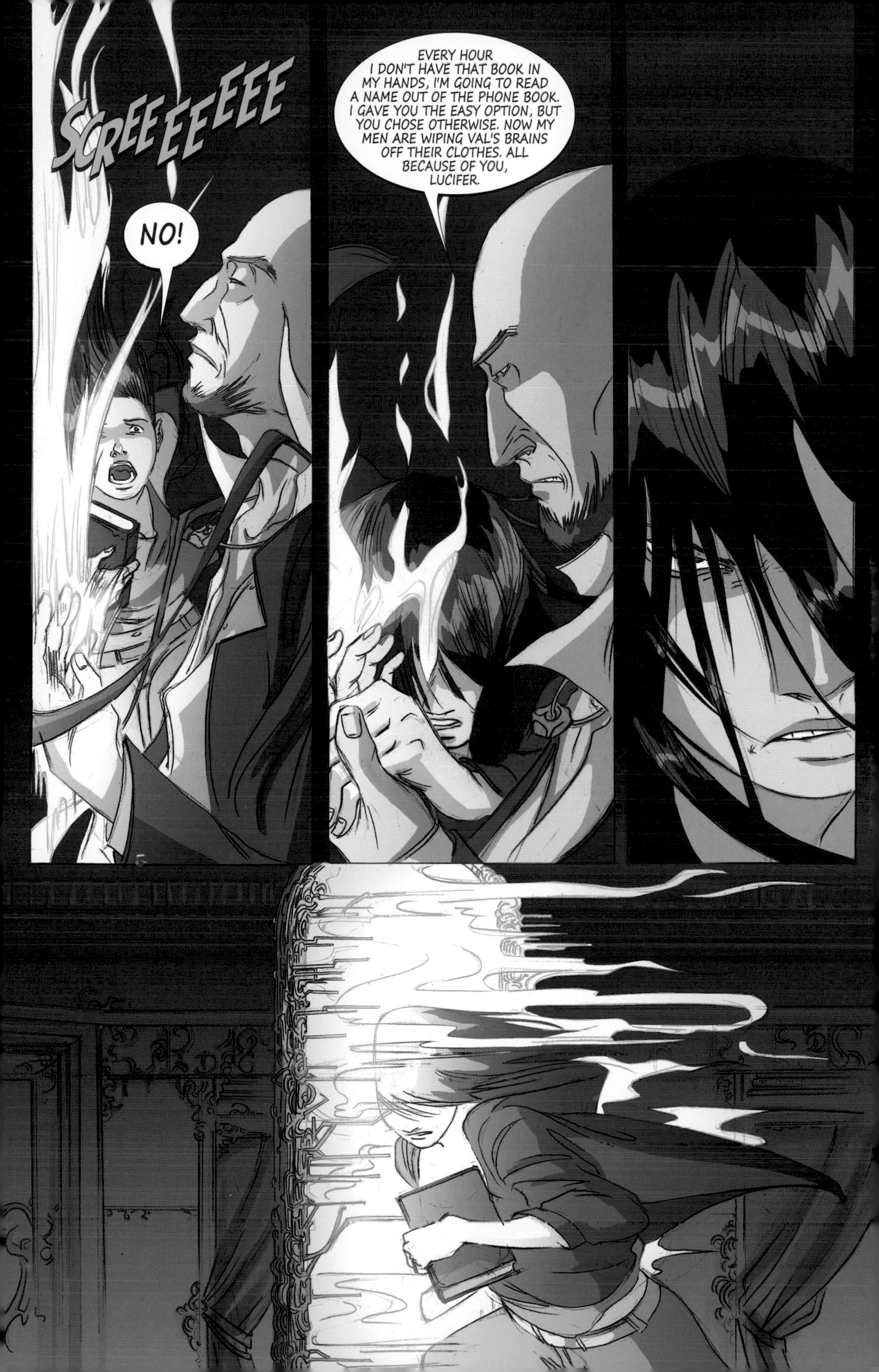
SCREEEEEEE
NO!
EVERY HOUR I DON'T HAVE THAT BOOK IN MY HANDS, I'M GOING TO READ A NAME OUT OF THE PHONE BOOK. I GAVE YOU THE EASY OPTION, BUT YOU CHOSE OTHERWISE. NOW MY MEN ARE WIPING VAL'S BRAINS OFF THEIR CLOTHES. ALL BECAUSE OF YOU, LUCIFER.

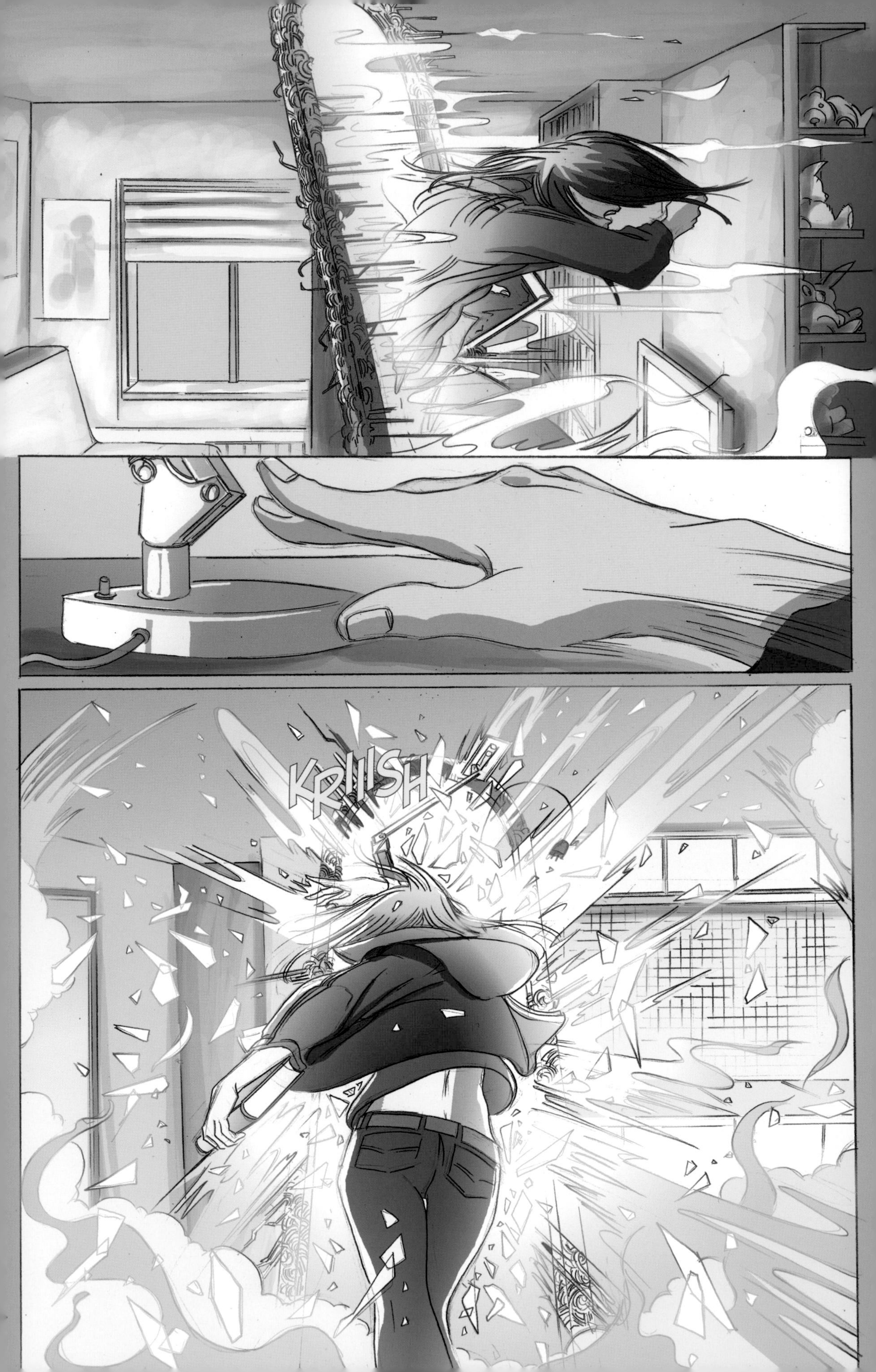
KRIISH

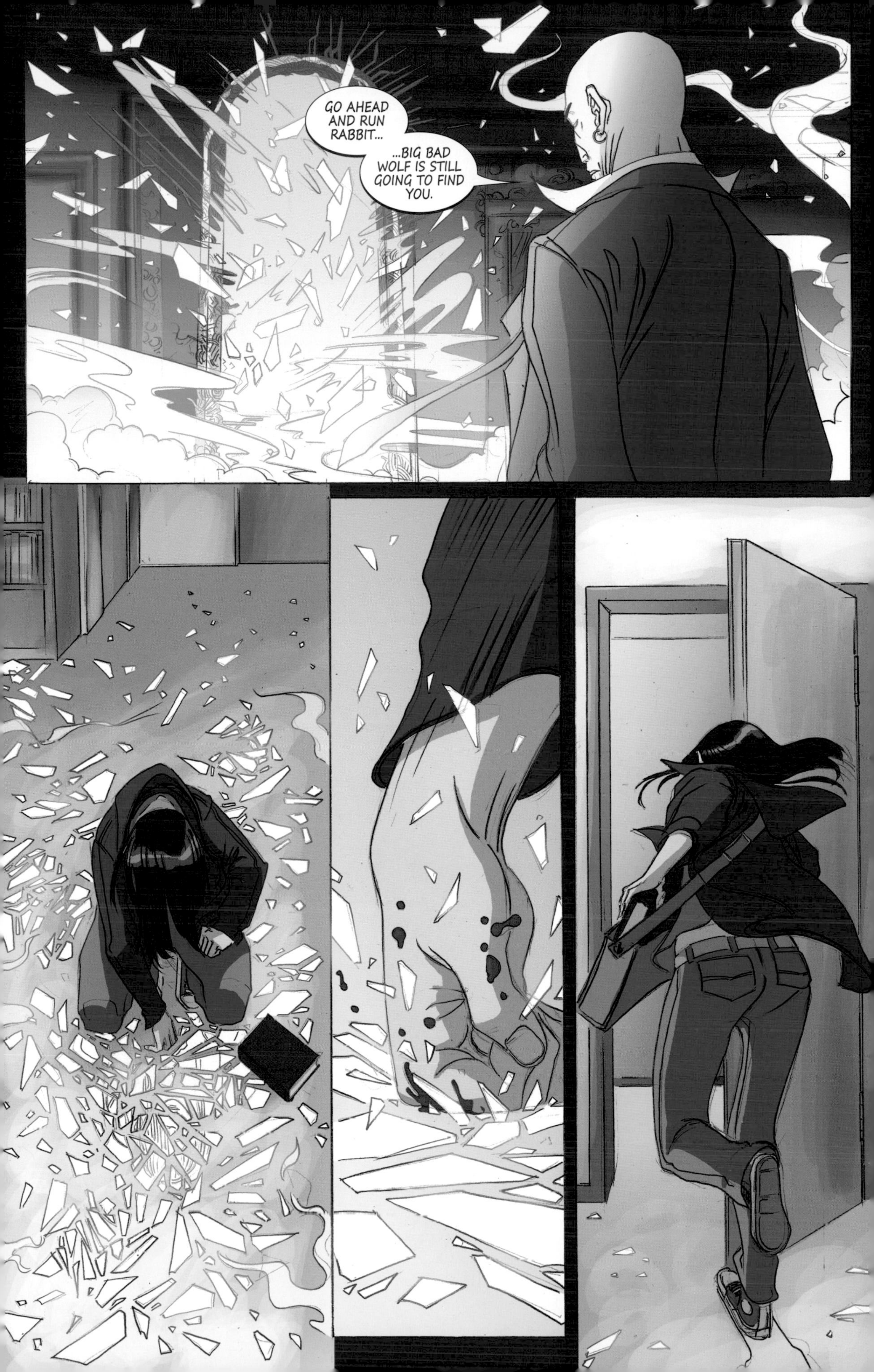
GO AHEAD AND RUN RABBIT...
...BIG BAD WOLF IS STILL GOING TO FIND YOU.

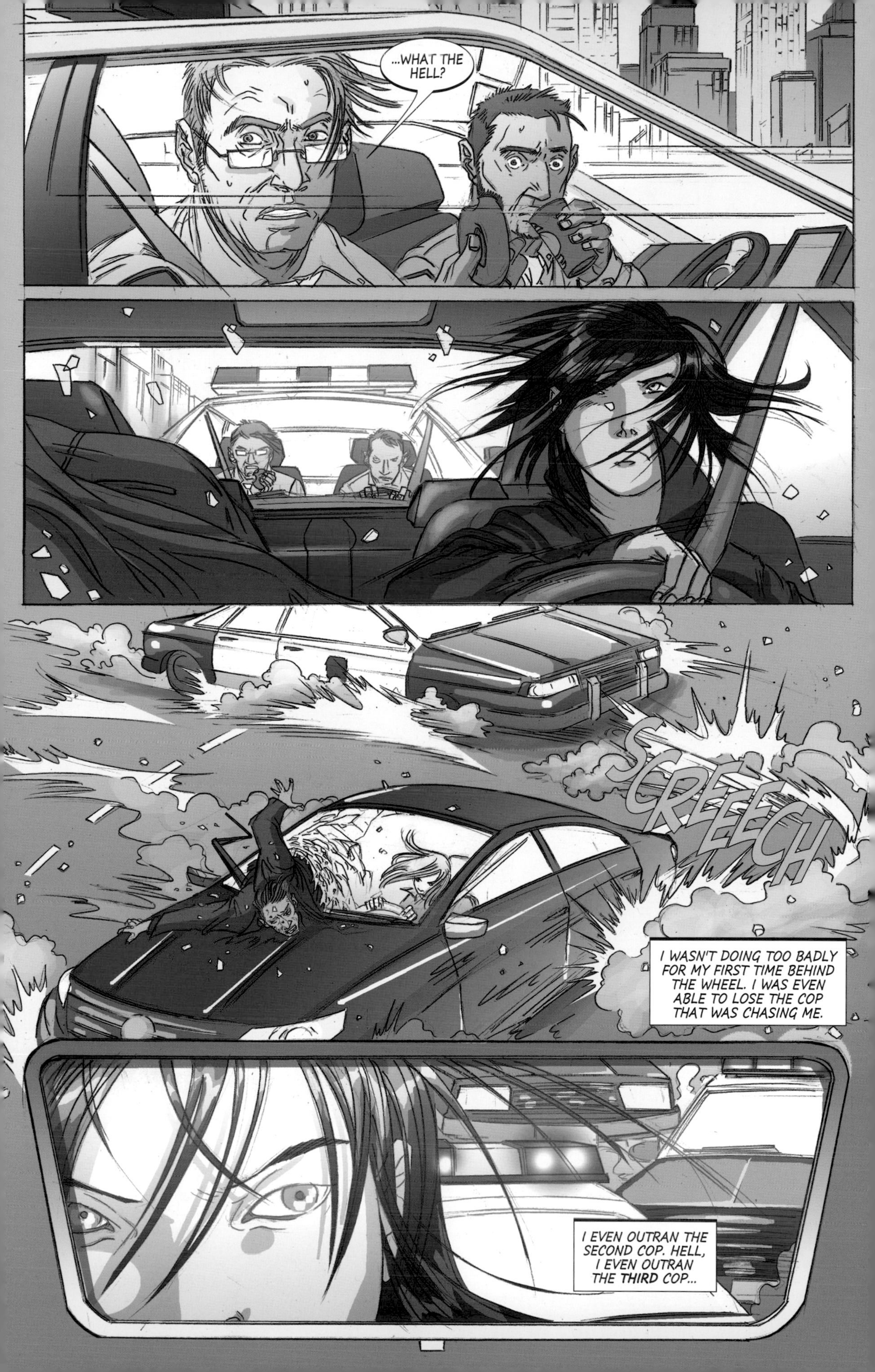
...WHAT THE HELL?
SCREEECH
I WASN'T DOING TOO BADLY FOR MY FIRST TIME BEHIND THE WHEEL. I WAS EVEN ABLE TO LOSE THE COP THAT WAS CHASING ME.
I EVEN OUTRAN THE SECOND COP. HELL, I EVEN OUTRAN THE THIRD COP...

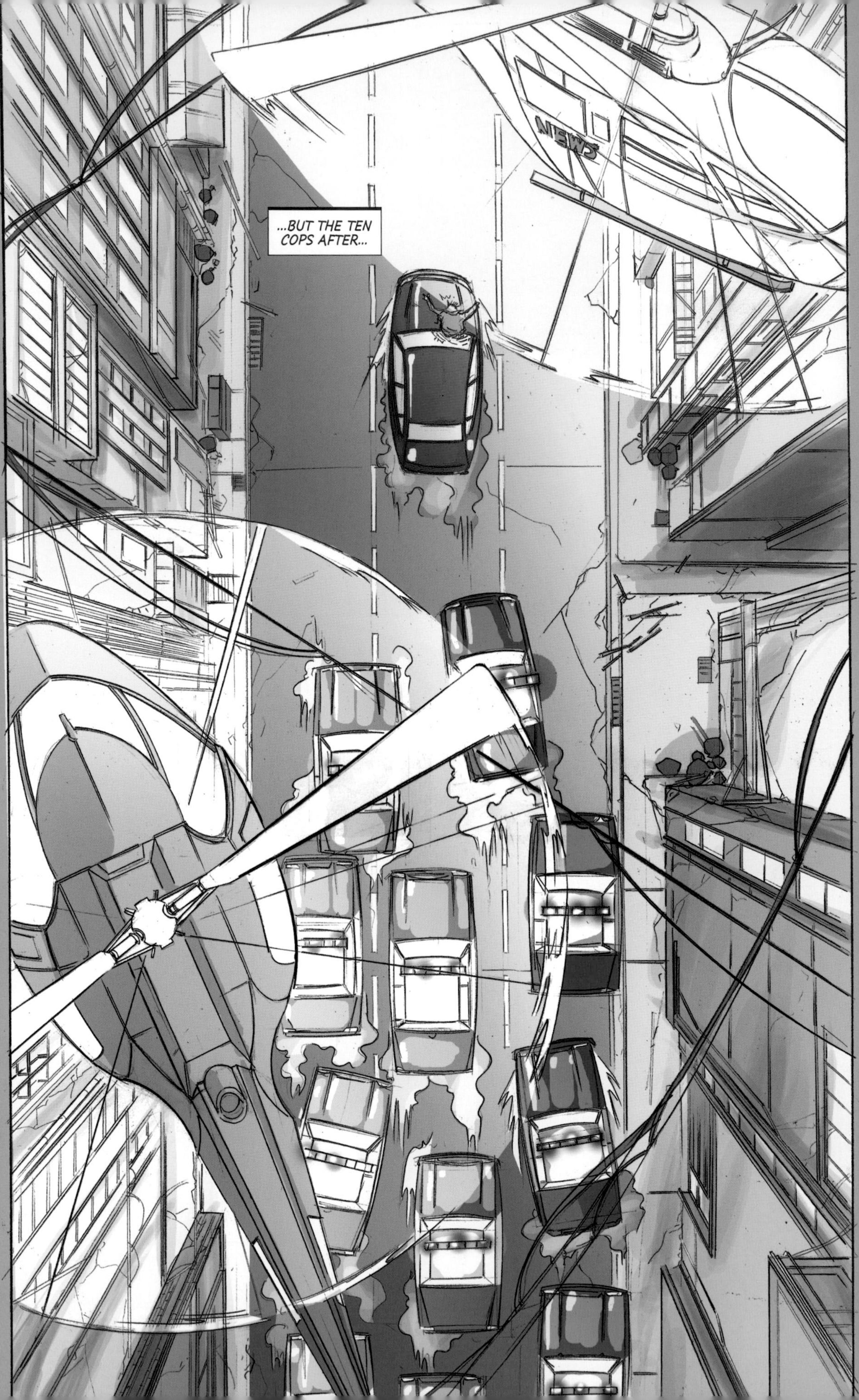
...BUT THE TEN
COPS AFTER...
NEWS

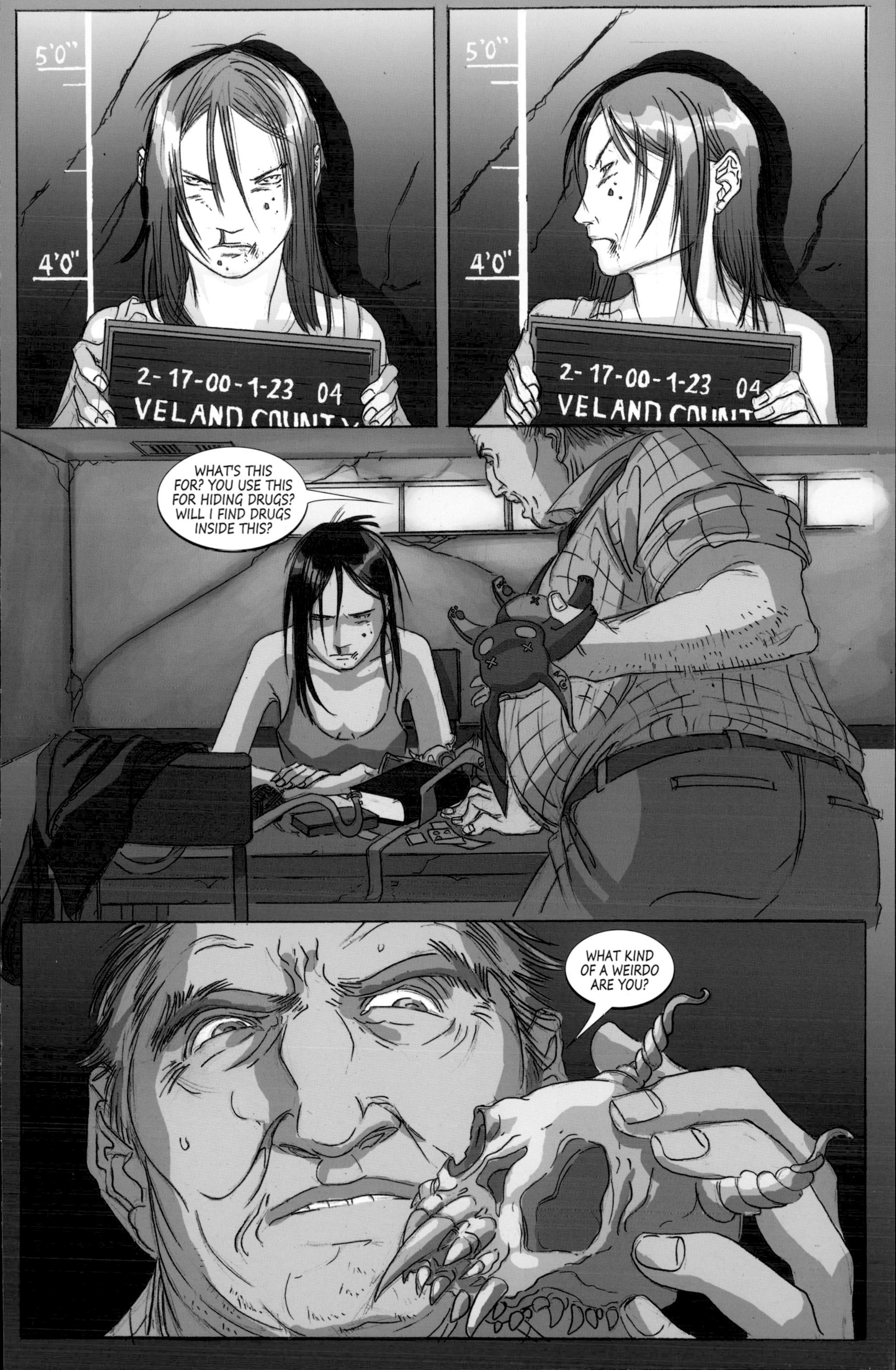
5'0"
4'0"
2-17-00-1-23 04
VELAND COUNTY
5'0"
4'0"
2-17-00-1-23 04
VELAND COUNT
WHAT'S THIS FOR? YOU USE THIS FOR HIDING DRUGS? WILL I FIND DRUGS INSIDE THIS?
WHAT KIND OF A WEIRDO ARE YOU?

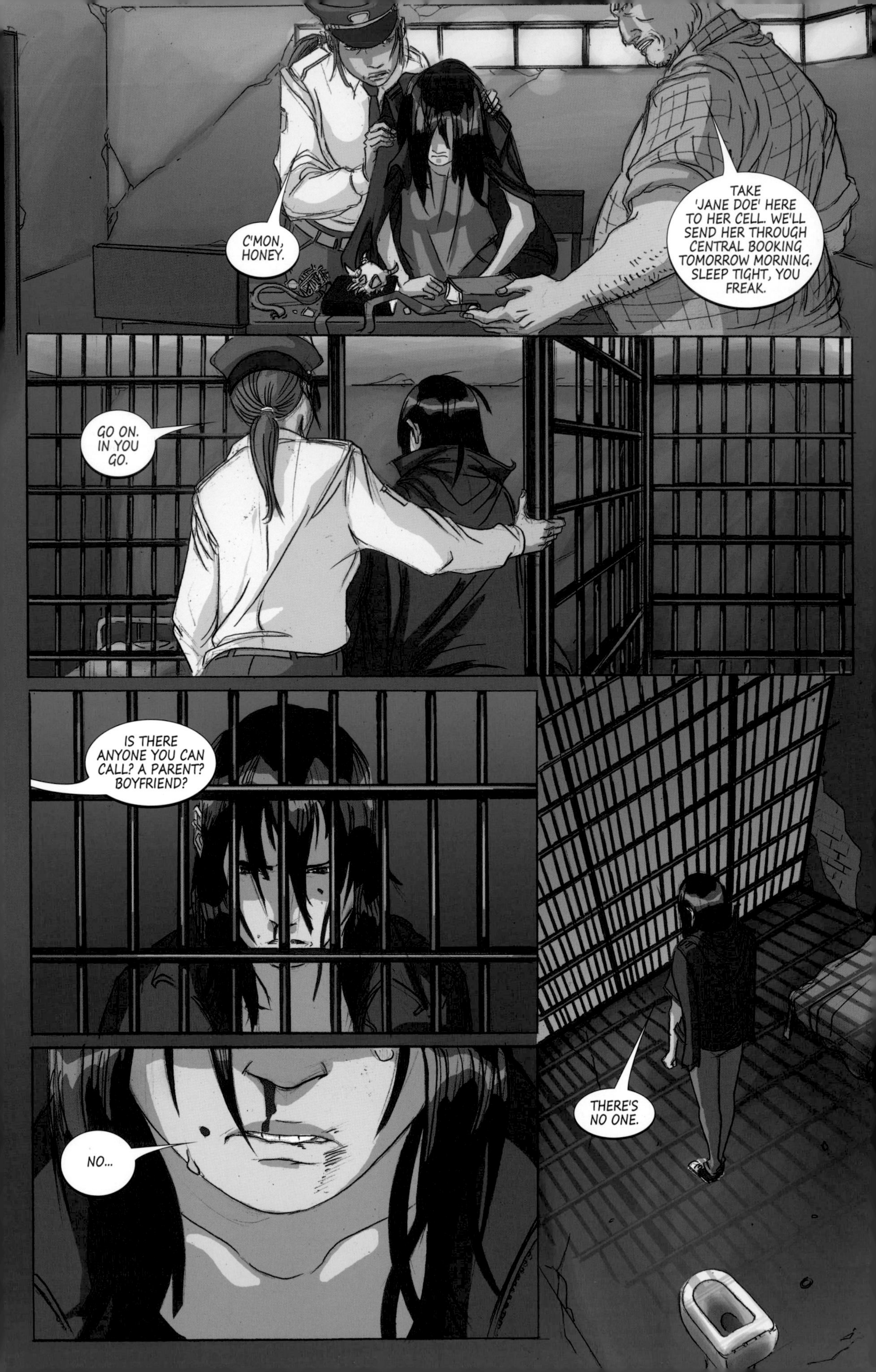
C'MON, HONEY.
TAKE 'JANE DOE' HERE TO HER CELL. WE'LL SEND HER THROUGH CENTRAL BOOKING TOMORROW MORNING. SLEEP TIGHT, YOU FREAK.
GO ON. IN YOU GO.
IS THERE ANYONE YOU CAN CALL? A PARENT? BOYFRIEND?
NO...
THERE'S NO ONE.

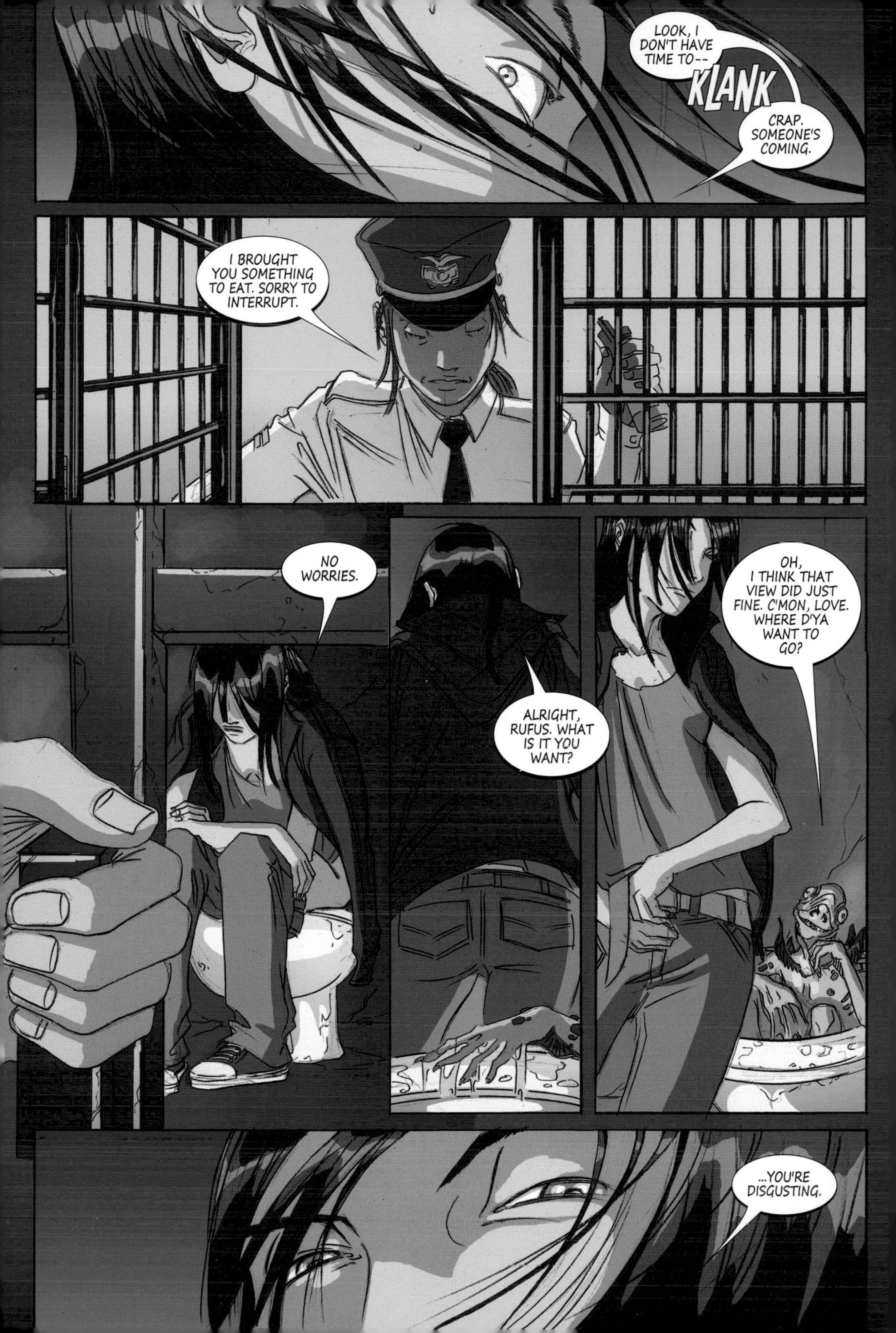
LOOK, I DON'T HAVE TIME TO--
KLANK
CRAP. SOMEONE'S COMING.
I BROUGHT YOU SOMETHING TO EAT. SORRY TO INTERRUPT.
NO WORRIES.
ALRIGHT, RUFUS. WHAT IS IT YOU WANT?
OH, I THINK THAT VIEW DID JUST FINE. C'MON, LOVE. WHERE D'YA WANT TO GO?
...YOU'RE DISGUSTING.

CHAPTER IV

WHEREIN LUCIFER BECOMES A DAY PLAYER AND FEARS THE NUMBER 30.

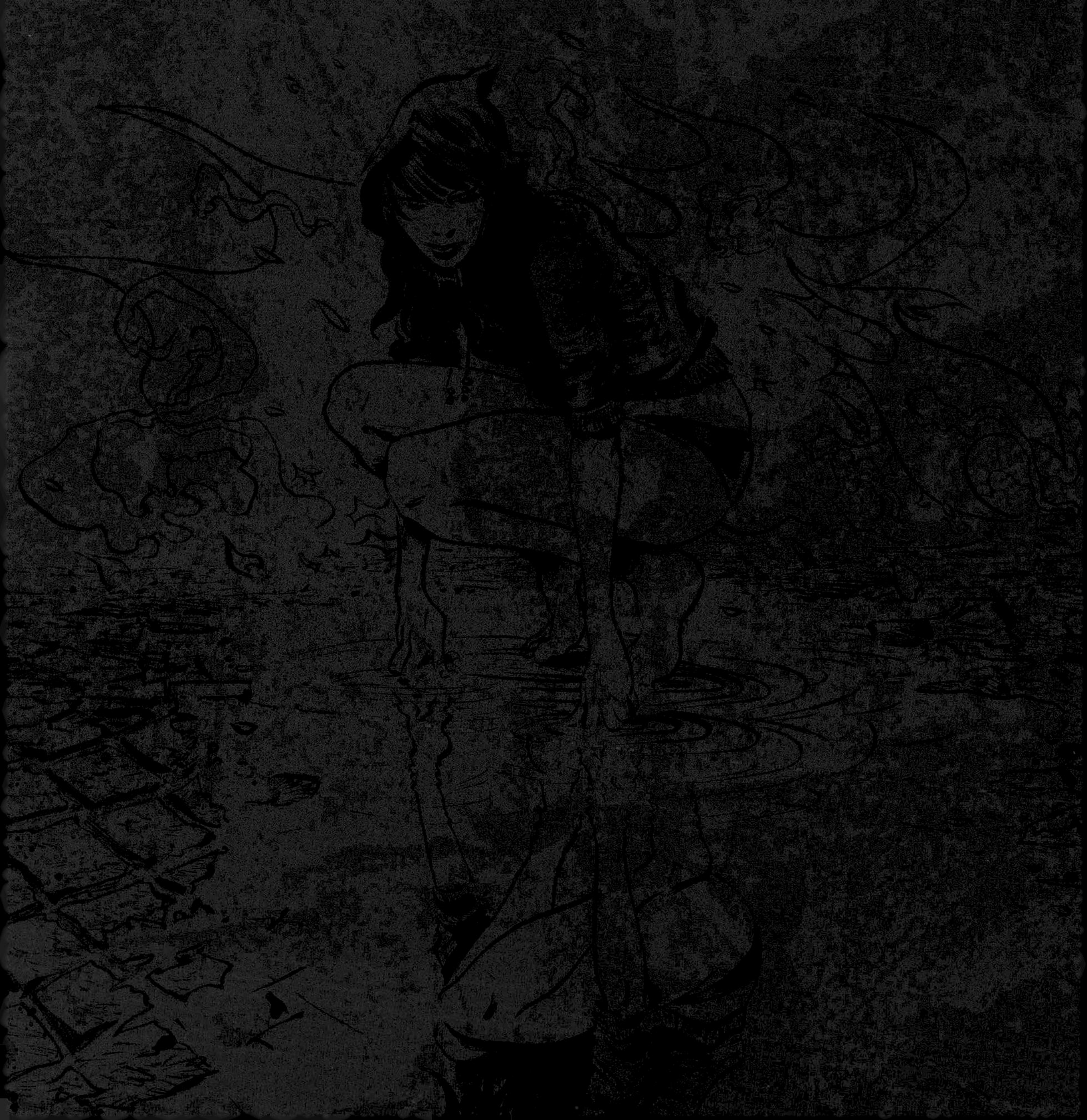

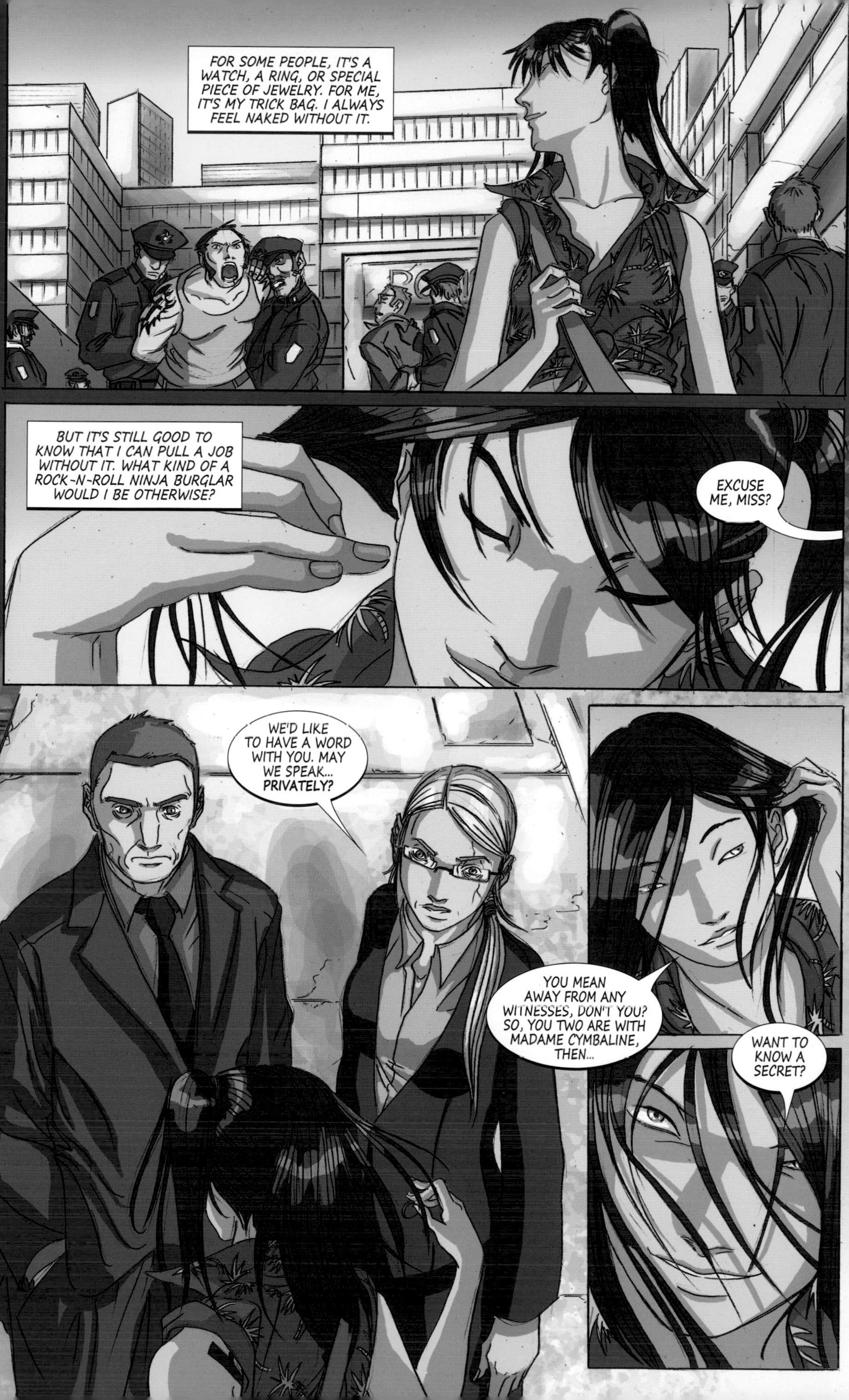
FOR SOME PEOPLE, IT'S A WATCH, A RING, OR SPECIAL PIECE OF JEWELRY. FOR ME, IT'S MY TRICK BAG. I ALWAYS FEEL NAKED WITHOUT IT.
BUT IT'S STILL GOOD TO KNOW THAT I CAN PULL A JOB WITHOUT IT. WHAT KIND OF A ROCK-N-ROLL NINJA BURGLAR WOULD I BE OTHERWISE?
EXCUSE ME, MISS?
WE'D LIKE TO HAVE A WORD WITH YOU. MAY WE SPEAK... PRIVATELY?
YOU MEAN AWAY FROM ANY WITNESSES, DON'T YOU? SO, YOU TWO ARE WITH MADAME CYMBALINE, THEN...
WANT TO KNOW A SECRET?

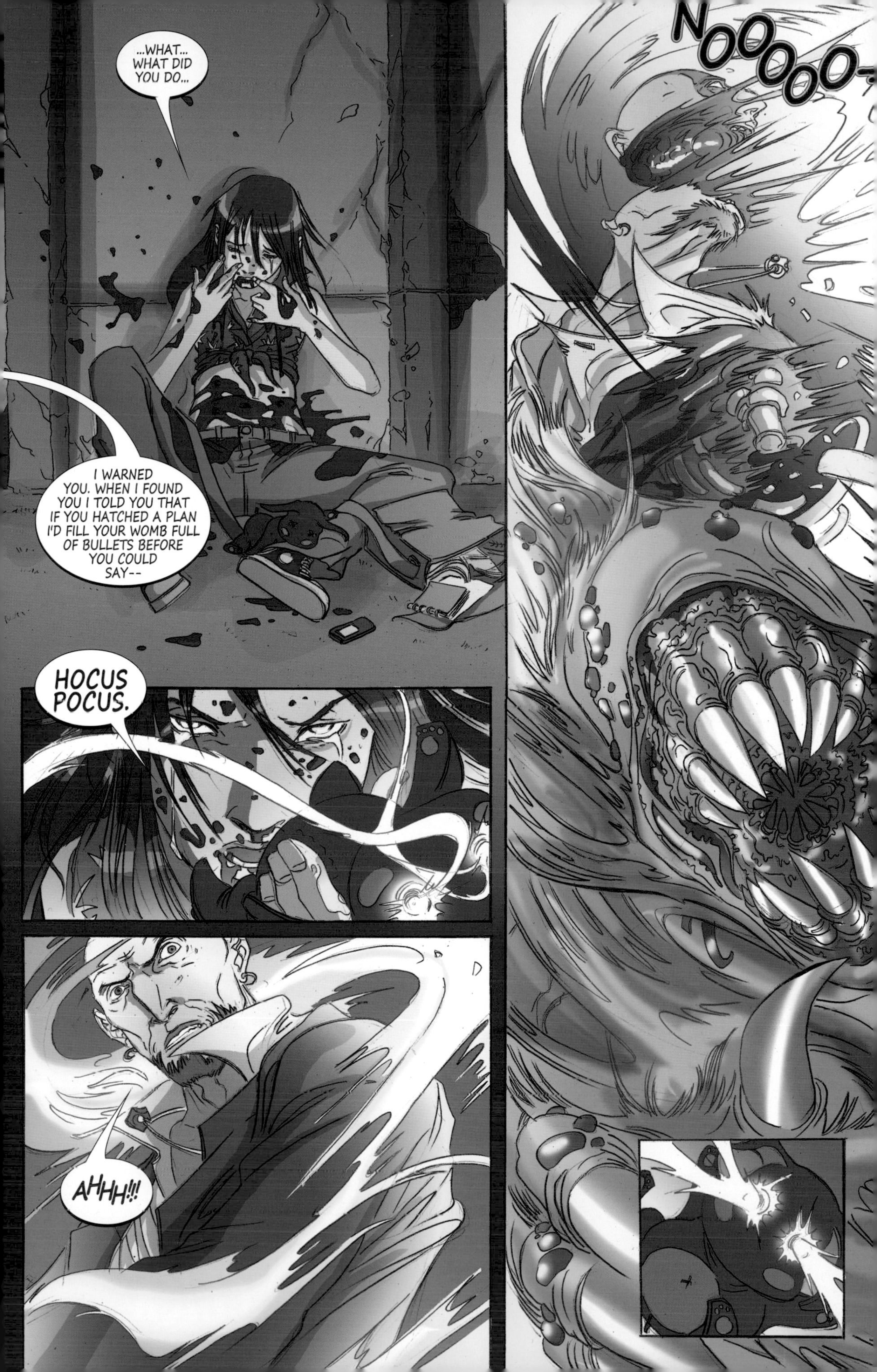
...WHAT...
WHAT DID
YOU DO...
I WARNED
YOU. WHEN I FOUND
YOU I TOLD YOU THAT
IF YOU HATCHED A PLAN
I'D FILL YOUR WOMB FULL
OF BULLETS BEFORE
YOU COULD
SAY--
HOCUS
POCUS.
AHHH!!!
NOOOOO--

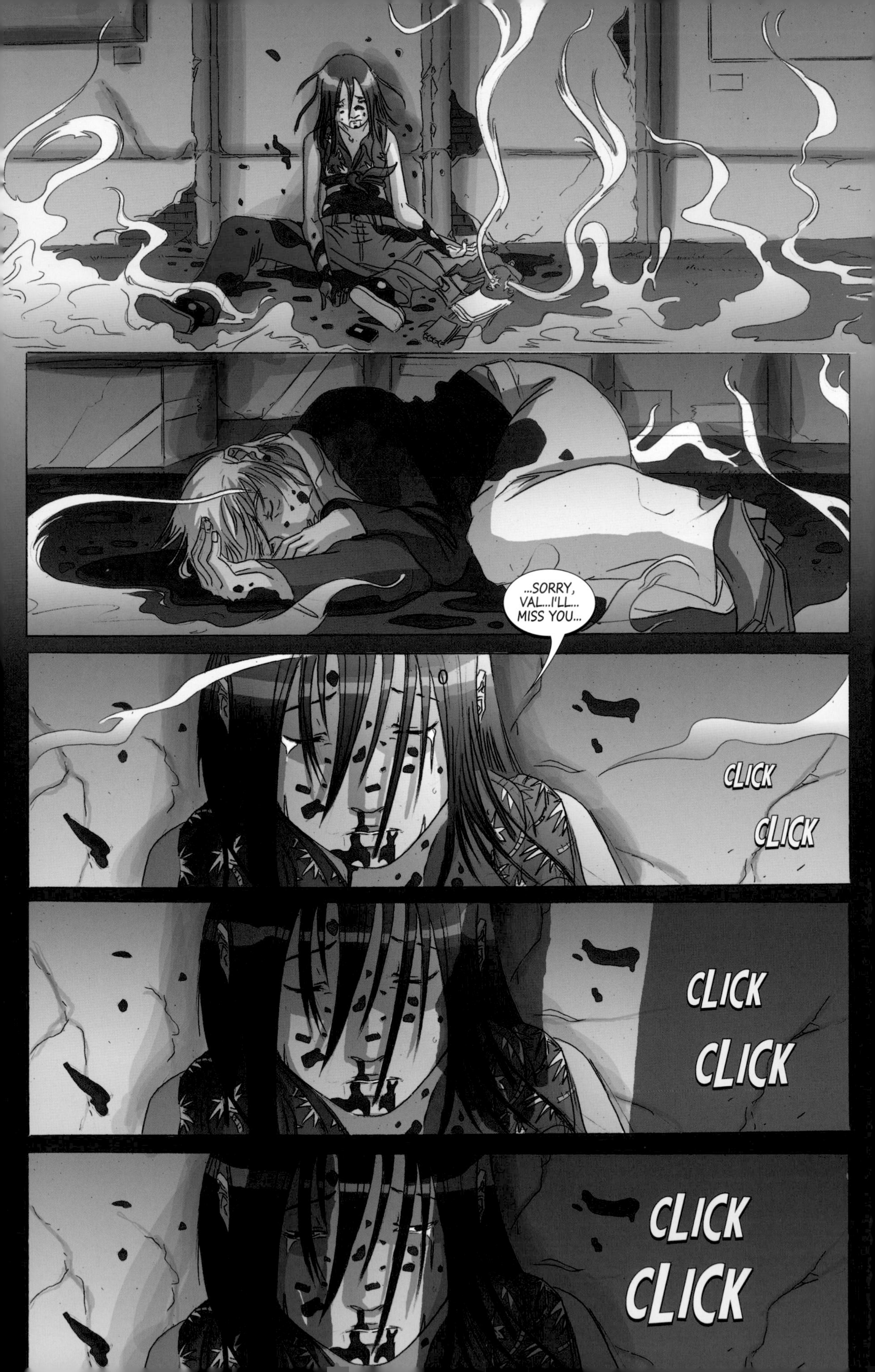
...SORRY, VAL...I'LL... MISS YOU...
CLICK
CLICK
CLICK
CLICK
CLICK
CLICK

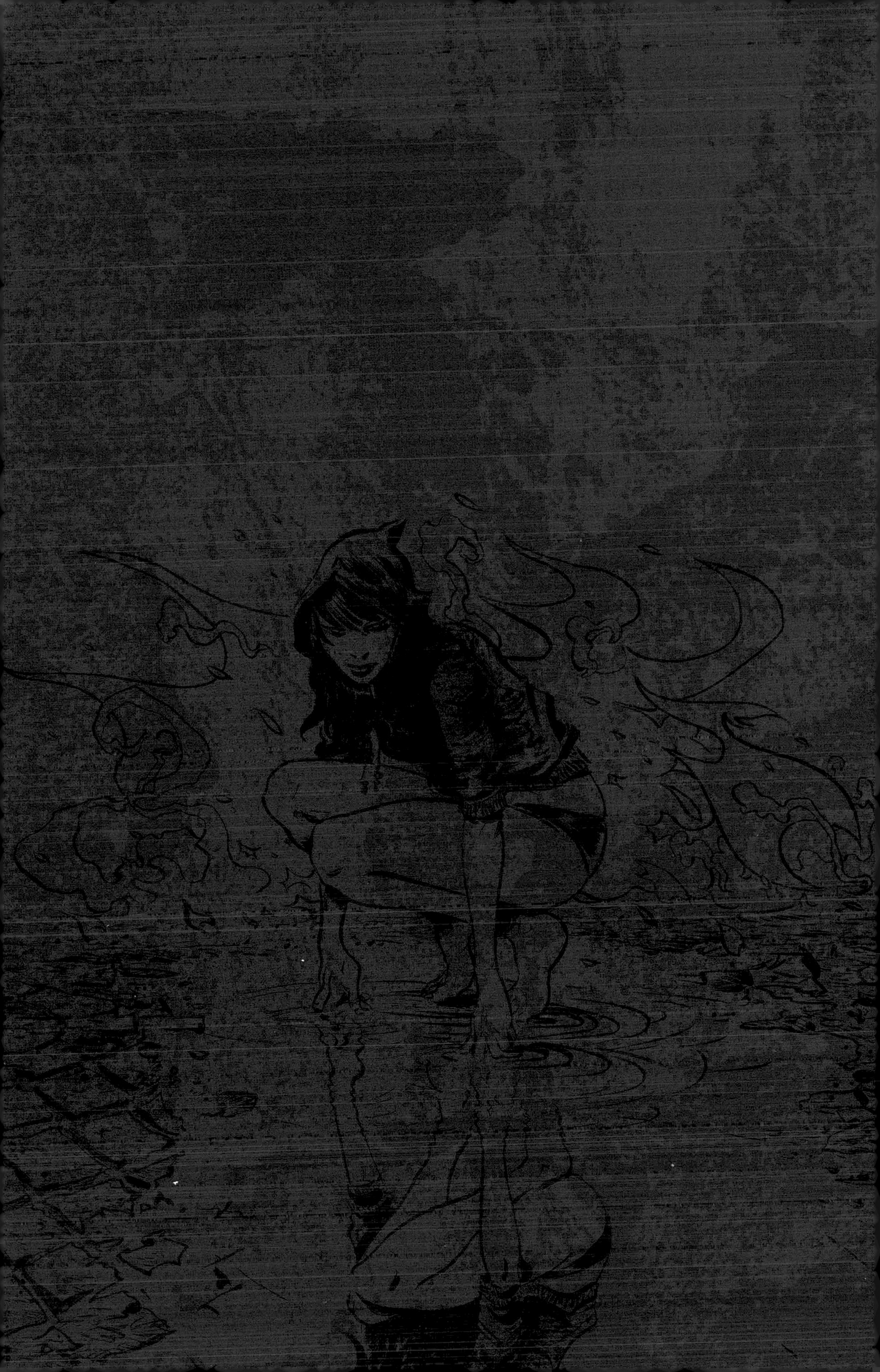

COVER GALLERY

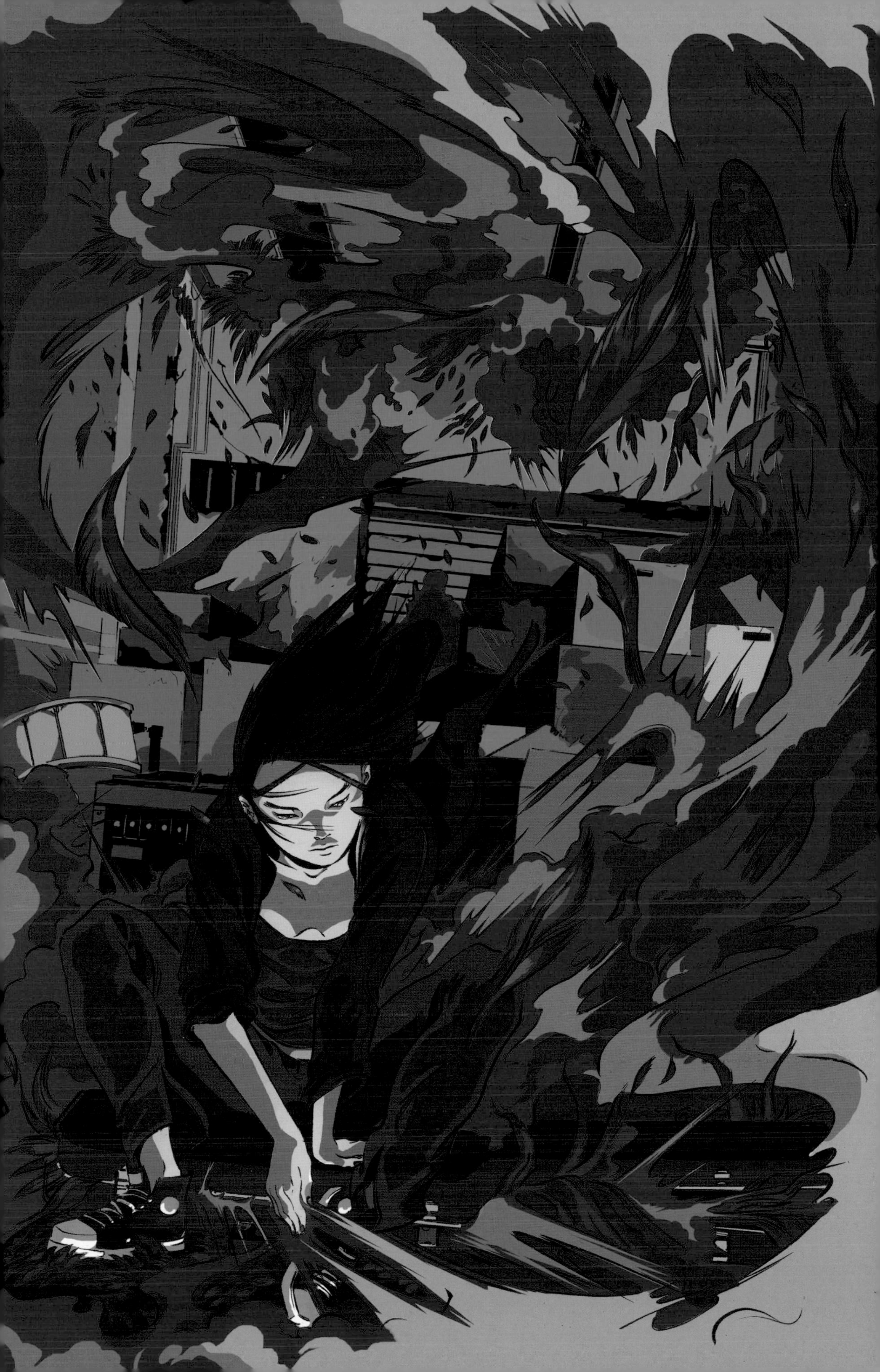

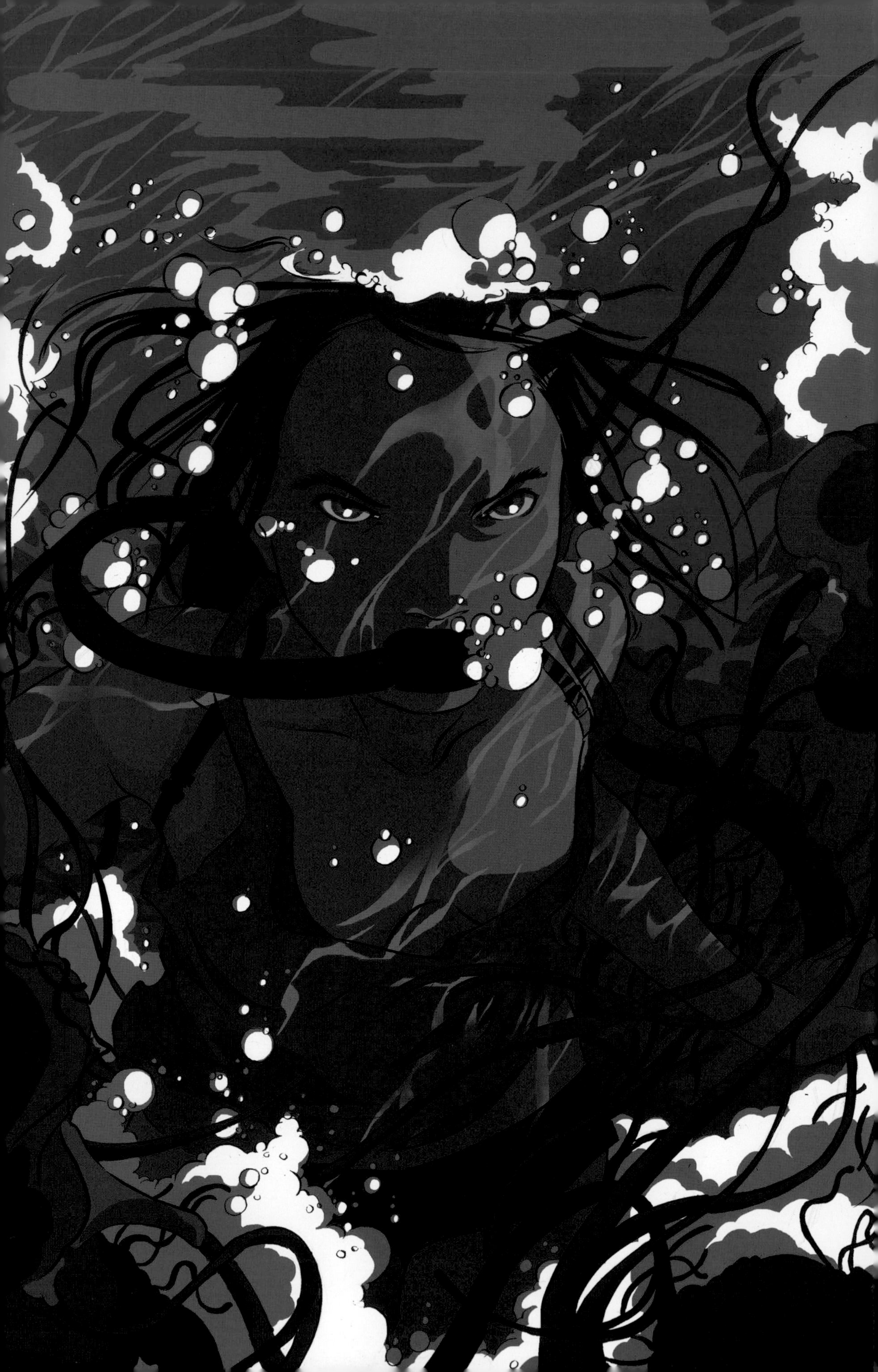

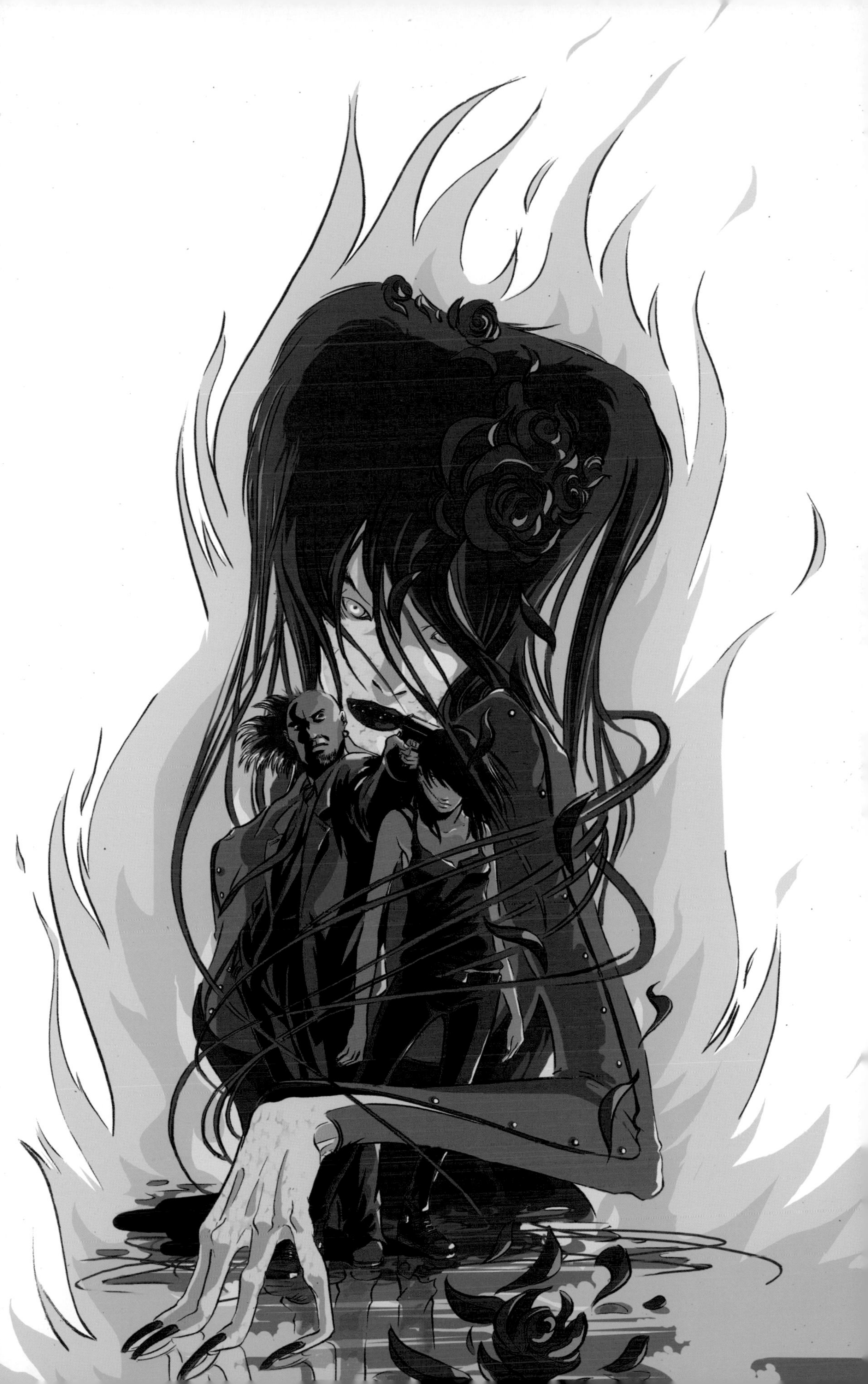

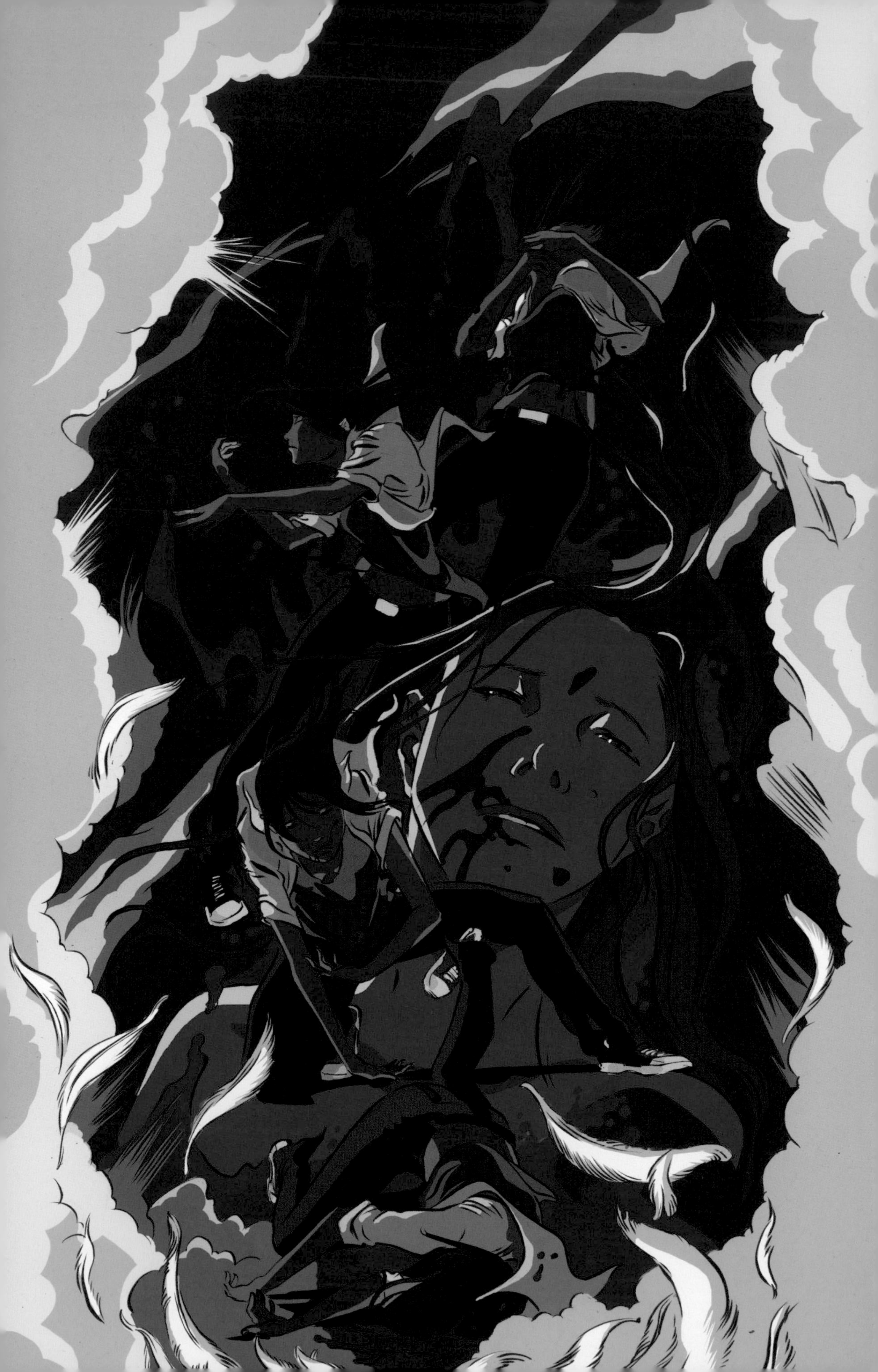

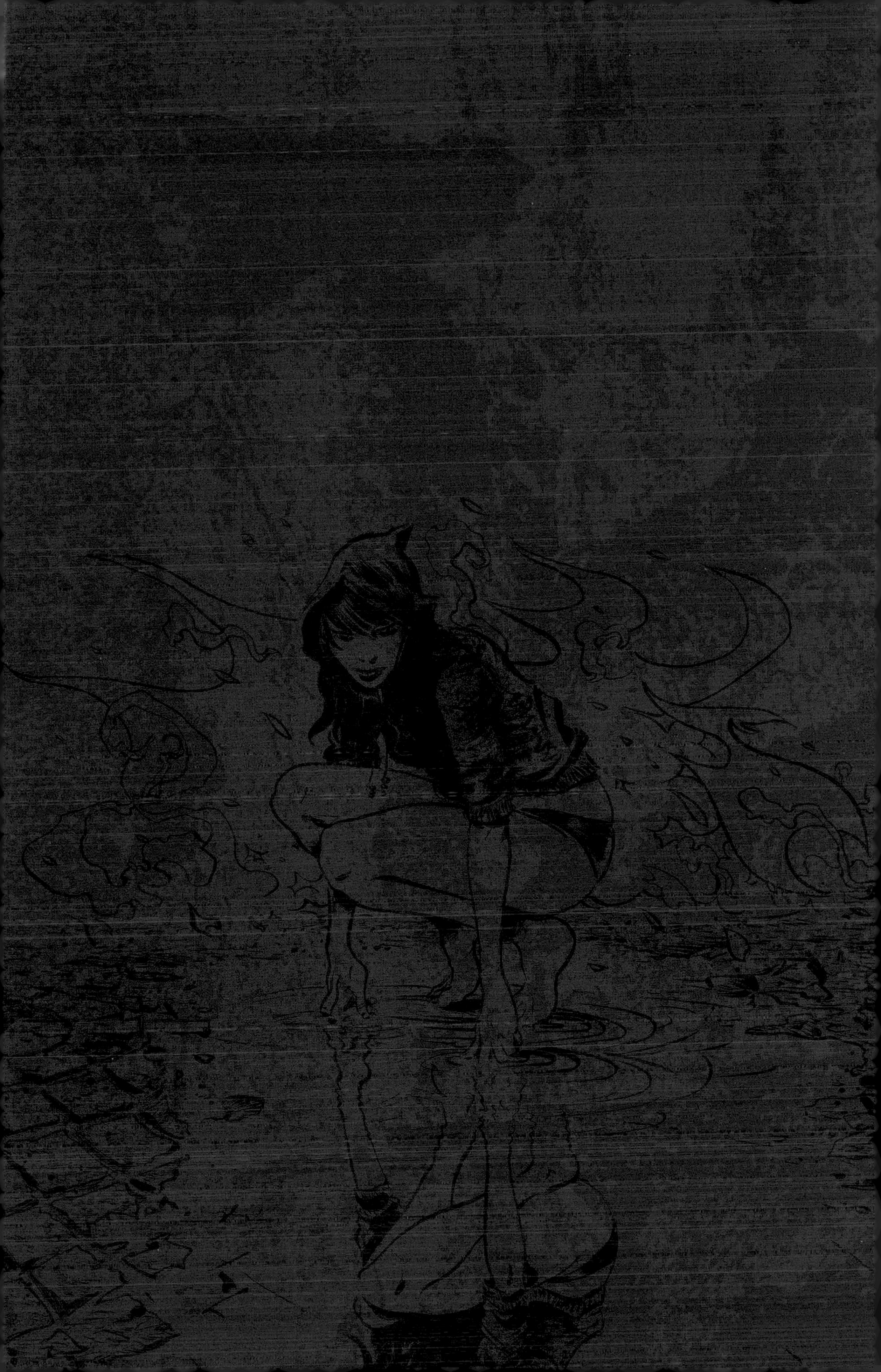

AFTERWORD

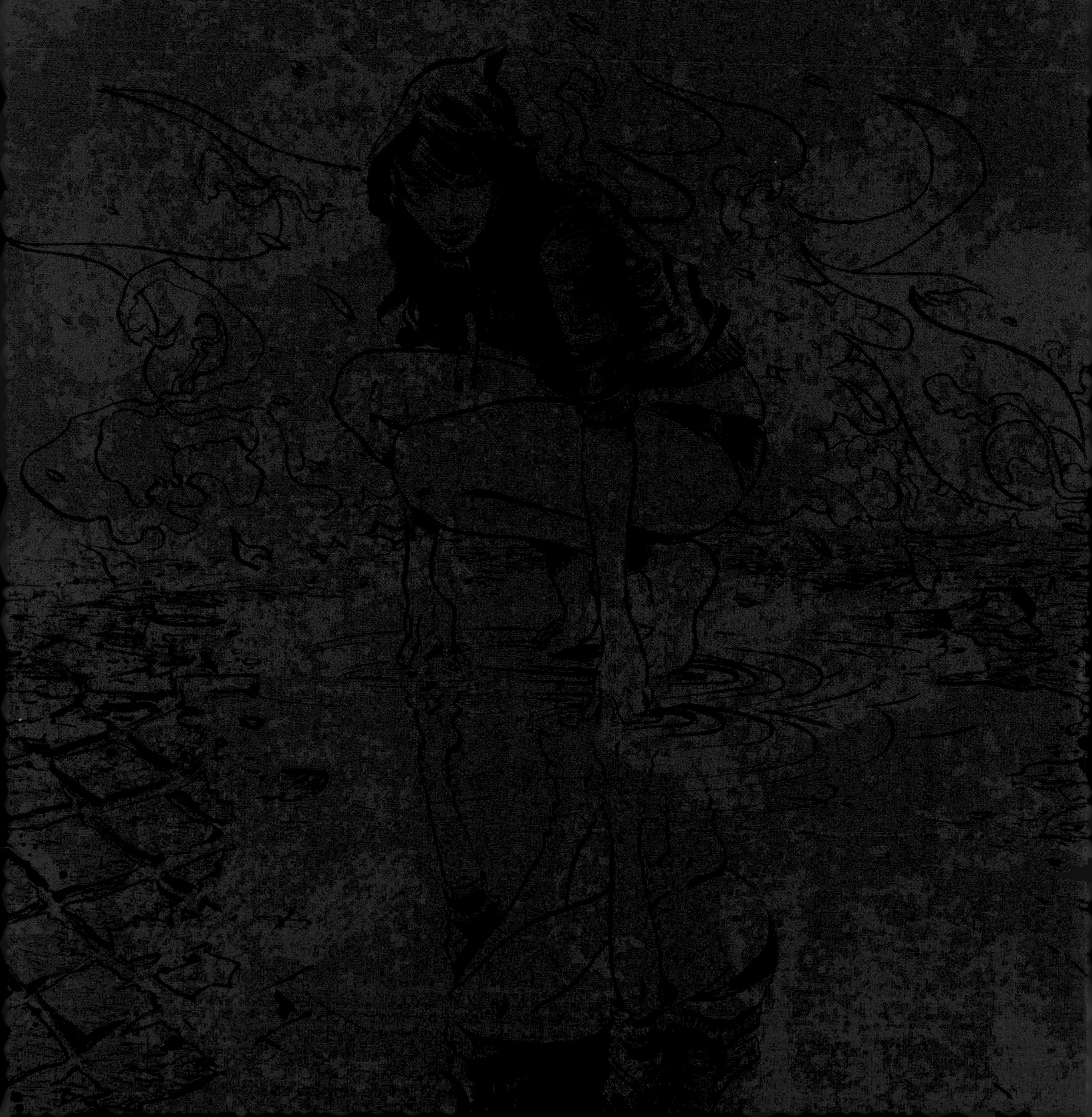

There's magic in the world.

That's quite a bold statement, I must admit, but it is, nevertheless, true. How do I know? You're holding the proof of it in your hands right now.

Alright, be honest. For a moment, you thought I meant the kind of magic that makes shapely assistants disappear, sends fireballs hurtling from one's fingertips, or binds ferocious witch-hounds inside pink and cuddly prisons. No, I'm talking about something else, something even more wondrous. I'm talking about the kind of magic that happens when an idea blossoms into something beyond even one's highest expectations. It doesn't happen very often, but when it does, it is, in the truest sense of the word, awesome.

The idea for the character Lucifer came to me in a fit of panic. I needed to think of some cover concepts for the third arc of my series FALL OF CTHULHU; but unfortunately, I wasn't sure what the story was going to be. Nothing was coming to me. Yet, as I tried to work a story through in my head, an image kept floating in my mind: there was a teen-aged girl sitting on the floor of a jail cell, drawing dark and ominous symbols in the dust around her. There she was, in my mind's eye, looking up at me as she scrawled runes on the floor, daring me to ask her questions. What did those symbols mean? Why was she in jail? And above all, who was she? For the life of me, I had no idea what my story was going to be, but I knew that it simply had to be about her.

As I developed her character and her story in FALL OF CTHULHU, Lucifer had become an amazingly rich and compelling character. She was strong, capable, and knew how to survive in a dangerous and terrifying world. And she did it all by herself. No super powers, no innate magical prowess, just her wits and the skills honed by the unforgiving mistress of necessity. And she had become more than just an interesting part of an ensemble that included deities with a fan base decades in the making. True to her name, Lucifer had become the star.

But she was a star in someone else's sky.

No matter how much I made FALL OF CTHULHU my own, how deeply I populated it with my own original characters, how much of my own voice shined through the story, I was still playing in Lovecraft's sandbox. Call it selfish, but I wanted Lucifer to walk in a world *wholly of my own creation, a place that wasn't so immured in shadow and despair. Rather, I saw her in a world with humor, compassion, and a beauty hidden beneath the horrors (it's no coincidence that Lucifer works for the curator of an art gallery). In short, I wanted the chance for Lucifer to have a happy ending. But it's one thing to talk about a world of beautiful horror. It's another to actually make one.*

That is, unless there's magic in the world.

Open this book up to any page and you can see the magic, weaving itself among the images, permeating through the paper like soft, cherubic whispers. Cris Peter's colors rise from the page like the grand finale of a master illusionist and every pencil

stroke sings the delicate song of a complex spell, proving that, without a doubt, Emma Rios is nothing short of a sorceress.

Emma and Cris gave HEXED a depth and vision beyond anything I could have hoped for. And they did it by doing what I thought was impossible: they created a world of beautiful horror.

My ego would love nothing more than to lie and tell you that it was I who had the inimitable vision to bring together these two sisters of the arcane. However, that honor belongs to my editor Matt Gagnon, a man who helped me shape this book into something more than just another story about a pretty girl fighting evil. He saw what HEXED could be and knew exactly how to make it happen.

It's a rare and wonderful thing when so many variables come together to make such a powerful piece of art. And I can think of no words exalted enough to praise the team that made HEXED into the stunningly beautiful story you hold in your hands. Because of them, HEXED is not just special.

It's **magical.**

Michael Alan Nelson
Los Angeles - July 2009